FUNDRAISING STRATEGY

Redmond Mullin

Second edition

Institute of

Dedication

To
Bartholomew and Frankie
Patrick and Carol
Sebastian and Benjamin
Frankie, Caedmon and Greg

The fundraising series
Community Fundraising Harry Brown (editor)
Corporate Fundraising Valerie Morton (editor)
Fundraising Databases Peter Flory
Fundraising Strategy Redmond Mullin
Legacy Fundraising Sebastian Wilberforce (editor)
Trust Fundraising Anthony Clay (editor)

First edition published 1997 by the Charities Aid Foundation (CAF)

Second edition published 2002 by the Directory of Social Change

Published by:
Directory of Social Change   Tel. 020 7209 5151
24 Stephenson Way   Fax 020 7391 4804
London   e-mail: books@dsc.org.uk
NW1 2DP   www.dsc.org.uk
from whom further copies and a full publications list are available.

The Directory of Social Change is a Registered Charity no. 800517

Design and production by Eugenie Dodd Typographics
Printed and bound by Bell & Bain Ltd, Glasgow

A catalogue record for this book is available from the British Library

ISBN 1 903991 22 6

Contents

Foreword

It will surely come as a considerable shock to many of the idealists in the not-for-profit sector to read that there is an analogy between military strategies and their fundraising strategies, and that both strategies are concerned with campaigns to win battles. However, the idealists can take comfort from the fact that their battle is not to subjugate an enemy but rather to win hearts, minds and support.

The commonality between military and not-for-profit sector strategies is that both are designed to achieve success and that to succeed requires a high measure of professionalism. In the not too distant past, there was a quite commonly held view in the not-for-profit sector that professionalism – or 'management' as it was more often disparagingly termed – had no place and was somehow harmful to the purity and idealism which were the lifeblood of the sector. Happily, there is now increasing recognition that idealism and good intentions are by themselves not enough and that the key to future success will be the results achieved for those for whose benefit the organisations exist. And, of course, while passion and commitment to ideals are the fuel which powers the sector, it is professionalism that achieves outstanding results.

Nowhere does this apply more than to fundraising – an area which seldom is given the recognition it deserves and where it is often necessary to confront another prejudice: that fundraising is a less worthy or prestigious job than fieldwork, research or service provision. Often the people working in these other fields seek to distance themselves from the fundraisers and fundraising in the belief that they have more important things to do. They tend to lose sight of the fact that, without the fundraisers, there would be no organisation at all.

The clear message that Redmond Mullin delivers is that fundraising is not only an integral part of every not-for-profit organisation, but that in order for fundraising to be successful it needs the commitment and involvement not only of the fundraisers but of everyone else in the organisation, whether they be trustees, staff, volunteers or supporters.

At Oxfam we seek to recognise this by our 'one programme' approach. We see all the work we do as part of a single programme, the constituent parts of which are interdependent and mutually supportive. Thus fundraising enables us to respond to humanitarian emergencies, our work on emergencies feeds through into our work on rehabilitation and development, and this grassroots work in turn provides credibility to our lobbying and campaigning work, all of which raises our profile and provides our fundraisers with the material and image they need to fundraise successfully. According to Oxfam we recognise that we all have a role to play in fundraising.

Fundraising is a demanding and difficult task not made any easier by the understandable wish of donors that as much as possible of their donations should reach the beneficiaries for whom it was intended. However, in the market-driven world in which not-for-profit organisations operate today, it is impossible to raise funds without investing in marketing and in people – both staff and volunteers – actually to do the work. Donors will only accept this if they can be satisfied that the investment made has produced an excellent return.

Redmond Mullin's book outlines what needs to be done to ensure that such an investment can produce the maximum return. It is based on his own wealth of experience as an acknowledged leader in the field of fundraising. It is illustrated by reference to the strategies followed in specific campaigns. It is about strategy, research, planning, focus, targeting and communication. Above all, it is about professionalism driven by a passion for a cause – which is, after all, why Redmond Mullin and all the other fundraisers work in the not-for-profit sector rather than applying their very marketable skills to maximising their earnings in the corporate world.

Joel Joffe
(Lord Joffe, CBE; Chairman, Oxfam 1985–1991)

Introduction

A definition of strategy as it applies to this book

Strategy is a word used with familiarity, but not necessarily with precision. The origin of the word is military, and its direct military applications, while they may change with situations, are generally clear: a set-piece battle differs from ambush or guerrilla warfare or a worldwide 'war' against terrorism. The analogy with military strategies has been usefully and exhaustively applied to business practice and marketing, sometimes with contrivance. The analogy has also been invoked extensively in discussion of fundraising, since there are differences, but few serious discontinuities, between marketing and fundraising. The military connections may be uncomfortable, but the principles and applications are relevant and useful. Many forms of planning – business, corporate, marketing and fundraising among them – overlap with strategic planning. This book will apply the analogy lightly, using it to clarify principle and process.

Within the analogy's broad terms, *strategy defines all points along the route (or the various routes), the equipment and support needed, and the timetable to get from a starting point to a determined destination*. This loose description contains some crucial ideas. When an organisation starts to plan ahead, it must begin from the place where it is. It is unconstructive to assume a desired, but unreal, starting point – perhaps that held by a competitor or antagonist – rather than the place it is at now. Organisations have to be equally clear about the planned destination. A wanderer may start a journey with no idea where it will end, happy in this ignorance; a strategist, with objects to achieve and resources to deploy, must know the destination or destinations intended. The wanderer may depend on happenstance to travel from here to an unknown place and to arrive at an unknown time; the strategist plans the route, the means, the timetable in terms of an intended achievement or place of arrival. Ulysses was a wanderer; astronauts depend on NASA strategists.

The argument of this book is not that luck does not happen. It is that luck happens to the prepared mind and that, to give high probability of success to most forms of fundraising, rigorous strategic planning is a prerequisite. Only through such planning can there be confidence that the processes selected to achieve a goal are apt, efficient and effective and that they will be delivered with the greatest possible cost benefit. This presupposes that a goal has been determined, relating funds raised to activity, service or some capital project. Without sound strategic planning the goal may eventually be reached, but at high cost and with waste of resources. Alternatively, in the absence of a well-plotted plan, the whole enterprise may be abandoned as impossible to achieve, or to achieve in time. And, as time goes on, it will be difficult to assess what the fundraising has achieved or where it is going, or the return on investment.

An outline of the book's structure

Chapters One and Two begin with a short discussion of the concept of strategy as it is applied to war, business and marketing, as well as to fundraising. There are differences and similarities in the application of the concept to these various operations, and there is detailed treatment of its relevance to not-for-profit bodies.

Chapters Three and Four deal with the planning process, creation of the strategic plan and implementation of the strategy. There is then an Interlude, which reviews the material and principles discussed to that point and prepares for what follows.

Chapters Five and Six describe and discuss application of these principles to a range of types and sizes of funding programmes, for a diversity of causes. The principles established are relevant to all types and sizes of not-for-profit body: large, national; small, local, specialised; concerned with welfare, health, education, the arts, sport or religion. However, the ways these principles are applied will vary. A national charity or institution which starts with many long-established friends or alumni and with potent patronage is in a very different situation from one which is new, small and local, perhaps dealing with an unpopular cause. Social-work, academic, medical and arts worlds have different cultures. The great, hierarchical organisations with distinguished boards, functional committees and a structured directorate have opportunities and problems distinctly removed from an organisation where the director is also its fundraiser and whose board consists, maybe, of families and carers or a few of the founder's friends. These chapters also discuss some programmes that have failed.

Chapters Seven and Eight illustrate the views of people who have experienced the strategic processes from a variety of viewpoints. It yields a range of interesting, useful but unrepresentative views. These lead on to the conclusions and prognostications of the last chapter.

The intended audience of this book

There are many reasons for fundraising successes and failures, beyond the basic factor of how much the public likes, dislikes or is familiar with a cause or service. Many of the factors can be influenced by the people involved – the staff, volunteers and the trustees.

An appeal has inauspicious prospects if its sole object is to raise money. Raising money is in itself value-free. An appeal aiming only for money is unlikely to create the charge of energy within and around the organisation which marks successful fundraising and goes on delivering results. Where the fundraising is the explicit enabling function of an organisation's service and shares its idealism, it satisfies donors and trustees – but fundraising is not magic. Lack of investment, failure of will, disengagement from action and responsibility by trustees and senior management are symptoms of a funding programme which is expected to deliver results through fundraisers' magic. Such programmes will not engage the major supporters closely who share in the delivery of the results during and after most large-scale appeals.

That account defines the people for whom this book is principally written:

- people who design and direct fundraising programmes;
- their senior management (if these are different people);
- the person who chairs the board and certain other trustees, who must be personally committed to the achievement of any major programme;
- the senior staff and volunteers who must manage implementation of the programme;
- occasionally, and in some special circumstances, a few major supporters.

It is the great ideas and ideals of an enterprise that will unite these disparate people. The funding programme, if planned and implemented appropriately, can realise these ideals.

What may seem unusual in that short list is the inclusion of major supporters. Such involvement can be mutually rewarding and productive, and it is discussed later. The role of trustees in strategic planning and decision-making is much more usual, but can be unsatisfactory and even counter-productive. Of course they must be involved: they have unalienable responsibility for what is decided and done within their organisations. The problems are that trustees may be too little informed or ill-equipped by training, temperament, and experience either to oversee the processes adequately or to take proper risks for attainment of their organisation's objects. This is partly a result of poor processes of selection (which may be based not on qualifications but on acquaintances and friendships), partly of the vagueness of their roles, partly because even the best qualified may suffer a loss of judgement when they become trustees.

Why read it?

The context for fundraising has changed in a few ways since the first edition of this book was published. Over the last ten years there have been many quite massive gifts from the new rich. There have also been many gifts above £100,000 from people who are not rich but whom I have described as 'prosperous'. The Lottery has settled in as a major funding source, sometimes over-demanding in the conditions it sets. Distractions from the Millennium have passed. The general climate for fundraising, and its background of fiscal provisions, remains positive. And all the centuries-old principles for fundraising remain valid. There are many opportunities.

So why a second edition of this book (apart from the fact that the first edition sold out)? Because the planning of effective fundraising and effective implementation of those plans are not just important. They are part of our society's health and wellbeing. If the cause for which we raise funds is of little importance, so is the fundraising for it; if it is of great importance, so is its fundraising; and the causes for which most of us work are highly important.

This means that all of us in fundraising have serious responsibility for being skilled, organised, creative and effective as we work to achieve planned outcomes, thus allowing luck to happen. In all this, while applying established principles, we must be flexible and sensitive, adjusting to changes in our contexts for fundraising. So a text on fundraising strategy must state principles but it too must allow for changes.

Fundraising is more art than science. Practitioners want guidelines, to know the stages of various fundraising procedures; but fundraising cannot become too mechanistic, or it will underachieve. It will fail to identify opportunity and exploit it responsively. It will not change the realities, because it applies the tested formulae too rigidly and accepts too readily what history and surveys argue to be the given truths. Nothing is, in that sense, 'given'. There is useful, successful experience to be observed. But the exceptional fundraiser can change the realities. The problem is that knowledge and skills can be taught; talent cannot. Talent is given.

Acknowledgements

My thanks to Lord (Joel) Joffe and to the contributors to Chapter Seven: Nick Booth and Giles Pegram from NSPCC, Christopher Carnie from The Factary, Mark Jefferies from Craigmyle, and an anonymous contributor. Gillian Gallagher and Elaine Dodds advised me on the text. Beyond anyone else, perhaps, I thank my assistant, Jackie Abey, who produced the document, managed its delivery and cajoled me while writing it. For this second edition, Janice Rylatt, who prepared the text for me.

Redmond Mullin
Chagford

Redmond Mullin MA, LicPhil, is chairman of Redmond Mullin Ltd. Formerly a Jesuit, he has been in research at Masius, in advertising at J Walter Thompson, in fundraising with Wells, a director at the Charities Aid Foundation, a non-executive director of the London Philharmonic Orchestra, and chairman of the Advisory Committee for the Open University Voluntary Sector Management Programme and ICFM's Fellows Working Party. He is a Trustee of Dartington Summer Arts Foundation. He has published, lectured and broadcast extensively on fundraising, and related and unrelated matters.

CHAPTER ONE

Military and business strategies

'Strategy' is originally a military concept. Authorities such as Sun Tzu and Clausewitz defined the art by which war could be used, with cost benefit, to achieve objectives defined by governments and rulers. The principles of strategic planning and action have been applied effectively to business and marketing. They apply equally to fundraising.

Military strategies

The *strategos* was commander of an army or of armies. In Byzantine Greece, the *strategoi* were high state officials. That is the ancient origin of the term. Somewhat more recently, Karl von Clausewitz (1780–1831), the great military strategic theorist, stated that: 'The strategist must . . . define an aim for the entire operational side of the war that will be in accordance with its purpose' (von Clausewitz, 1832).

This chapter begins with the original, military concept of strategy because, by analogy, it clarifies discussion of fundraising strategies. Fundraisers do not aim to vanquish enemies, destroy armies, occupy territory. However, they do mount campaigns to defeat the competition and to win the hearts and minds – and a dependable proportion of the means – of their funding prospects and supporters. The analogy with war is imperfect but enlightening.

This chapter provides a survey (but not an exhaustive study) of useful points from military strategy, drawing from four principal, classic sources:

- Sun Tzu's recorded statements in *The Art of War*, dating from about 500 BC.
- Niccolò Machiavelli's *The Art of War* (1521), the only work of his that was published during his lifetime.

- Karl von Clausewitz's *On War* written in 1819, published posthumously (1832).
- Baron Henri de Jomini's *The Art of War* (1838).

All four authorities lived through massive conflicts: Sun Tzu lived in the Era of Warring States, Machiavelli in Renaissance North Italy; Clausewitz and Jomini had senior active and strategic roles in Napoleon's wars, the latter adding to experience by switching sides. There are points on which all four agree, as well as interesting differences, but their main arguments are clear, and some of these will be applied to the exposition of fundraising strategies.

Going to war

Sun Tzu insists that you do not go to war because you are angry. Famously, Clausewitz saw war as 'an act of policy': 'a true political instrument, a continuation of political intercourse, carried on with other means'. So 'once it has been determined, from the political conditions, what a war is meant to achieve and what it can achieve, it is easy to chart the course'. The objects of a war are defined through discourse between, on the one hand, the ruler, prince or government, who decide the objectives and, on the other, the military commanders, who must operate within the restraints of the quality, numbers and resources of the forces available to them. According to Jomini, 'the first care of [an army's] commander should be to agree with the head of the state upon the character of the war'.

Military strategists argue that wars should be started only with clear goals and understanding of what they are to achieve. According to Clausewitz, the strategist must 'draft the plan of war, and the aim will determine the series of actions intended to achieve it: he will in fact shape the individual campaigns and, within these, decide on the individual engagements.' 'We have seen', writes Jomini, 'that, in the most important operations in war, strategy fixes the direction of movements, and that we depend upon tactics for their execution.'

Planning a military strategy

As in fundraising, planning depends on good intelligence and information, gained through all kinds of means, including patrols, reconnaissance and spies. Sun Tzu writes that '. . . the commander must thoroughly acquaint himself beforehand with the maps so that he knows dangerous places', while Jomini asserts that a general should multiply '. . . the means of obtaining information for, no matter how imperfect and contradictory they may be, the truth may often be sifted from them.' Machiavelli says that a general should have around him 'a sort of council' made up of wise, well-informed, trusted men from whom he 'may learn not only the state of his own army; but also that of his enemy's' and who will 'well consider the nature of the terrain where they are; whether it is most advantageous to the enemy or themselves'. The aim is to know the enemy's numbers, minds, intentions, morale.

However, as Jomini warns, 'Perfect reliance should be placed on none of these means [for gathering information]', and Sun Tzu shows both how to deduce events from such signs as rising dust, the way an envoy speaks, noise from the enemy camp, movements of birds and also how to deceive. Clausewitz is eloquent on the uncertainty of information received: 'The only situation a commander can know fully is his own; his opponent's he can know only from imperfect intelligence . . . Since all information and assumptions are open to doubt, and with chance at work everywhere, the commander continually finds that things are not as he expected . . . War is the realm of uncertainty', with three-quarters of the factors affecting it 'wrapped in a fog of greater or lesser uncertainty . . . War is the realm of chance.' There are limits to the rational conduct of war.

The art of leadership

Planning and the gathering of information are essential, but, as Clausewitz says, the process should not lead us into 'a dreary labyrinth . . . a nightmare in which one tried in vain to bridge the gulf, between [an] abstract basis and the facts of life'. War is more art than science, a 'part of a man's social existence', engaging intellect, psyche and idealism. Hence the crucial role of the commander, who must combine genius, creativity and boldness with the ability, given the best possible information and a sound plan of action, to interpret at a glance how situations and opportunities are developing. The commander must show outstanding leadership: according to Jomini, he should 'do everything to electrify his own soldiers, and to impart to them his enthusiasm . . . The greater or less activity and boldness of the commanders of the armies are elements of success and failure, which cannot be submitted to rules.' The general must know how to arrange a good plan of operations, and how to carry it to a successful termination.

That account of war adds a new and interesting element: leadership, morale and idealism are presented as factors inspiring to the army. Machiavelli, mentioning the things to be admired in the old Romans, gives this list: 'To honour and reward *virtu*; not to scorn poverty; to value good order and discipline in their armies; to oblige citizens to love one another, to decline faction, and to prefer the good of the public to any private interest; and other such principles which would be compatible enough with these times.' This introduces idealism and morale as complementary factors, a point taken up by Jomini: 'The *morale* of an army and its chief officers has an influence on the fate of a war; and this seems to be due to a certain physical effect produced by the moral cause.' Clausewitz is even stronger: '. . . the moral elements are among the most important in war. They constitute the spirit that permeates war as a whole, and at an early stage they establish a close affinity with the will that moves and leads the whole mass of force, practically merging with it, since the will is itself a moral quantity . . . [although] next to nothing can be said about these things in books, they can no more be omitted from the theory of the art of war than can any of the other components of war.'

Once in the field, commanders should be left alone by the politicians: 'No evil is greater than commands of the sovereign from the court . . . He whose generals are able and not interfered with by the sovereign will be victorious.' As Sun Tzu puts it, 'When you see the right cause, act; do not wait for orders.'

The hierarchy of levels between planning and execution can be summarised thus:

Strategic $\rightarrow$ operational $\rightarrow$ tactical

That may look straightforward, but, as Clausewitz said, 'Everything in strategy is very simple, but that does not mean it is very easy.'

Strategic planning for companies

There are evident differences between military and corporate strategies. Companies are in competition but not at war with each other, except through an exaggeration of poetic licence. However, there are also important points of similarity, particularly in the planning stages of strategy.

A company exists to generate profits, for its own growth and development, for the benefit of shareholders and its other stakeholders, such as employees. As with an army, it has an objective or objectives, determined by its board with their senior managers; and these objectives will in turn be shaped by a combination of external and internal factors. An established group will have an historically determined position in the markets and in the public's perception. Decisions on objectives may be complex, affected by financial factors such as profits, return on investment, policies for diversification and growth – and by non-financial factors such as public responsibility, philanthropy, the company's behaviour as a good corporate citizen. Corporate or product image, style and positioning are influential. Decisions are further complicated by the personal objectives of people within the company, which might relate to earnings, profit sharing, equity, benefits, status.

All these factors may influence the decisions that are taken, but the frame within which these decisions are taken should be the strategic plan; and the continuing planning process may itself help re-define corporate, product or service objectives.

The corporate planning process: analysis

Corporate strategy provides some relevant points that are worth considering at this point. Assuming that the planning process starts from now, the company must start from its current objectives and performance and its competitive situation. It should be possible to describe what kind of organisation it is and to state its corporate, product and service objectives. However, it may be more difficult to measure how well the company is meeting its objectives or, for example, how well these objectives are understood and the extent to which they are recognised by staff, including senior executives. Does a shared vision and mission permeate the organisation? In what ways might this be relevant to clients or customers?

The effect of external factors

There are external and internal aspects to the analysis of a company's present position. External enquiry will consider the market or markets in which the company operates, their realised and potential sizes, in terms of corporate positioning, product or service penetration and performance, the main market segments and niches of opportunity. The planning exercise will also consider the broader environment in which the company and its competitors operate and will operate. This takes into account government regulations and policies, economic and demographic statistics and forecasts, threatened European Union (EU) regulations and other worldwide factors such as war, famine, drought, commodity prices, and also less tangible matters such as public opinion, fashion, moral and ethical values.

External circumstances change and have impact. The oil crisis in 1973 affected markets worldwide. When, in the 1960s, the taste of younger drinkers shifted to lager, Guinness had to reposition its stout in the beer market and introduce a lager of its own. Recessions destroy businesses, can freeze the housing market, and squeeze profits. Changes in retailing affected not only small shops but also giants like Woolworth and Littlewoods, who were in danger of being by-passed as new trends and prosperity swept shoppers up and away. Littlewoods has been hurt by the National Lottery. Activists and opinion have attacked the fur trade in Britain but not yet in Russia. BSE has destroyed our beef trade in Europe. Boycotts harm farmers and wine growers.

The consideration of internal aspects

Internal enquiry will consider factors ranging from the quality and performance of staff and management, remuneration and productivity, communication and motivation to IT, plant, investment, and locations. What are the company's main assets and skills? What are its shortcomings? Could additional or new resources improve performance and efficiency? There also has to be consideration of distribution and the availability of products and services, the awareness and understanding of customers or clients, their loyalties and behaviour as consumers. What features of the company, its products or services give it unique (the company hopes) competitive advantages?

The judgements that are made will depend on the company concerned: a major national operator with one or many leading brands will operate differently from a small, specialised operator supplying a niche market. With customer care, for example, complaints may be dealt with effectively almost regardless of brand or company size, but styles of personal cultivation of customer loyalty will vary enormously. There are very different opportunities in relation to a toothpaste, a corner shop, a supermarket which offers loyalty cards, the *Reader's Digest* which tries to make you feel personally valued and the broker, accountant or hotel by whom you are taken to the races, a match or dinner. One of the less tangible factors to be considered is the style of management and the quality of leadership at all levels within the company.

These enquiries are not merely abstract. They have practical conclusions. For example, a fresh description of the market as it is today and of the actual and possible situation of the company, product or service within it can lead to a re-definition of objectives. This happened with Guinness, Woolworth and the building societies; it could affect product range, pricing, marketing, packaging, the introduction of new products or the acquisition or sale of a company or product line. Related to these will be decisions on investments and the return over time to be delivered from them. The various methods chosen to deliver the objectives, their sequence in time and the synergy between them will be key elements in the strategic plan.

Commercial strategic planning in summary

The planning process will have drawn on interviews, focus groups, market research and audits to establish the findings and the margins of error qualifying them. The external analysis will have appraised the market and environment, the competition, the customers, the unrealised opportunities; the internal analysis will have looked at sales, profits, shareholders, customer loyalty and satisfaction, the capabilities and weaknesses of staff, management and the organisation as a whole. Options will have been assessed against each other, and the corporate mission re-defined or refurbished. The board, senior management and other staff will, ideally, have been involved, as well as external agencies.

This whole process will, however, have been barren unless guided by a vision that embraces values as well as profits. Customers will therefore have been a crucial focus for the exercise leading to the strategy. From the strategy the operational plan will now be developed, detailing the actions needed to deliver the strategy.

FIGURE 1 SUMMARY OF PLANNING PROCESS

Description of where the company is now
↓
Analysis of opportunities, threats, strengths
↓
Expression of vision and mission
↓
Establishment of strategic options and selection between them
↓
Determination of strategic intention
↓
Definition of the strategy and decision on investment
↓
Establishment and implementation of the operating plan
↓
Review and renewal of the process

The original, military concept of strategy can therefore be seen to clarify procedures and practice when it is applied to business. Both in turn clarify applications of the concept in the operations of not-for-profit organisations, as the chapters that follow shall demonstrate by analysis and illustration.

CHAPTER TWO

Not-for-profit strategies

Strategic planning for fundraising in not-for-profit organisations touches all key people involved. The strategy is to achieve the ideals of the organisation by engaging voluntary support, and the idealism of these supporters. The strategy must be realistic in terms of the external factors, which define the context for fundraising, and the factors internal to the organisation, which may determine its capabilities for service as for fundraising.

Preliminaries

Most of the organisations for which this book is written have explicit starting points for strategic planning: the *objects* stated in their trust deeds are interpreted by the policies of the board or trustees who have ultimate responsibility for all aspects of the organisation's operations and who determine the charity's *objectives* at a particular time. The strategic planning process may itself, as with a company, change those policies. It may even suggest a change of objects. For example, once polio had been eliminated in the UK, Action Research decided not to close down, but to concentrate on research into other disablements of children. However, the starting point for strategic planning is the approved objects and the current policies (where relevant with reference to a founder's statements), which provide a base on and from which developments can be built. The world is likely to have changed since those original objects, and even the current policies, were defined. Why today will an organisation start to plot tomorrow's strategy? Perhaps because the context has changed, because there is a special occasion, because there is an urgent need for funds, because strategic planning is a continuing, cyclical process. Or perhaps someone was suddenly struck by a vision of what should be.

Who should be involved in the planning process?

The planning processes should involve the trustees, the chief executive and the directorate or senior management, perhaps some outsiders. The trustees can delegate the work to staff or consultants but cannot shed responsibility for the policies and decisions which result. It may be that trustees will have to be persuaded by staff better informed and more motivated than they are to undertake the strategic study and carry out its conclusions. This in no way alters the trustees' essential roles and ultimate responsibility.

Issues of morale, competition and security may mean that the strategic planning process itself, as well as the information and proposals it generates, have to be confidential beyond the trustees and others who must be involved so that outcomes are not pre-empted and competitors alerted. If this is the case, the way in which staff and volunteers more generally will in due course be informed about significant outcomes may be an aspect of the plan.

Idealism and vision: the essential ingredients of the planning process

Unlike the armies or companies, the not-for-profit organisation engaged in strategic planning does not aim at victory or profit or fundraising for its own sake. Just as you should not go to war out of anger, you should not fundraise from greed. The planning starts from the organisation's objects, establishing what it should and could do to achieve these more efficiently and effectively. The intention is that those to be served should benefit, not the organisation for its own sake. The justification for any consequent appeal is that the funding requirement stems from the new vision and mission *as these relate to services*. Idealism is entailed for fundraising as it is for service.

Much that follows in this and the next chapter could be seen as routine. An organisation's intention might be to create an operation optimally efficient at generating funds; but good fundraising, while being efficient and effective, must be more than merely mechanical. To be successful with donors, the strategy must be charged with passion and idealism, for there was passion in the creation of most not-for-profit organisations discussed here. An arbitrary selection, taken from this century, might provide the following: Lillian Baylis for the arts; Cicely Saunders for the hospice movement; A S Neill for education; the small group that founded Oxfam out of its meetings in the Old Library of the University Church and the Quaker Meeting House in Oxford during 1942, before third world relief as we know it had become fashionable.

Of course, not all founders were flawless idealists: Barnardo was something of a rogue; Cecil Jackson-Cole (of Oxfam, Voluntary and Christian Service, Help the Aged) could be wilfully dictatorial; the same might equally be said of Mother Theresa. And motivations may be mixed and not purely idealistic: Alberti, arguing in his *Ten Books on Architecture* for the establishment of 'noble Hospitals, built at vast expense, where as well Strangers as Natives are furnished plentifully with all manner of Necessities for their Cure', adds a second motive: 'And by this Means these poor wretches did not wander about begging Relief, perhaps in vain' and the City was not offended by the 'miserable and filthy objects'.

There are echoes of such attitudes towards the homeless in Britain's cities today. Such cynicism is, however, rare. Benjamin Waugh's declaration in establishing the NSPCC is a better model: 'We don't want to do *something* for children, we want to do absolutely the best we can.' In subsequent planning exercises, the NSPCC has returned to its founder's statements, to see how in changed circumstances, with new structures, procedures, resources and shifts in statutory provision, children can be better protected, and child abuse outlawed.

In whatever field – reforming an orchestra or reshaping a charity's welfare delivery or re-equipping a university – the aim has to be the improvement and extension of services, inspired by a renewed vision. This relates to what Clausewitz says about the moral elements in war, which constitute the spirit that permeates the whole. The same kind of spirit needs to permeate a not-for-profit organisation.

TOPIC SUMMARY **VISION**

To be visionary is to be far-sighted, seeing beyond routines to the greater achievements which could and should be undertaken. By stating a vision the organisation – or more realistically its leadership – declares how it can better, more justly, more effectively realise its ideals and the objects for which it was established. In the practical context of strategic planning, this must be an exercise in ambitious realism not rhetoric. Looking beyond the horizon currently delimiting the organisation's terrain, the vision declares the attainable, if challenging, goals that are over that horizon.

So the vision statement is idealistic and challenging; but it declares the aims that the organisation *should* adopt and which are attainable by it.

So while strategic planning has practical objects – renewed and extended services usually demand significant increases in funding – the planning process can also renew the organisation's inspiration or spirit. Only part of this might depend on a return to origins (which has been a feature in the periodic reforms of religious orders). Part depends on seeing what the needs demand and what should be expected from the organisation today and for the years immediately ahead. Part depends on the leadership in and around the organisation concerned.

Finally, when the strategic processes have been completed, trustees and management will have choices to make between options for stasis or change. There will inevitably be risk in the choices. Strategic planning can reduce, measure, even control risk but cannot eliminate it, any more than it can reduce the more and less fortunate impacts of chance.

Strategic planning: external factors

As with a company, there are external and internal aspects to the analysis of a not-for-profit organisation's present position. External factors include the broad field of operation, the economic environment, competition, the legal and tax requirements, and public opinion.

The nature of the cause

One starting point for planning is the cause or field with which the organisation is concerned. This may at first be simple to define: the organisation is concerned with epilepsy, schizophrenia, heart disease or cancer, the protection of children or the environment, the health of the people of Whitechapel or the spirituality of the people of this parish, the provision of opera or of a sports facility, the operation of a great national art gallery or the creation of a small one, the future of an established university or the creation of a new one. The definitions become quickly more complex, with important implications for decisions on services to be provided and on fundraising.

For example, if we look further at some of the arbitrarily selected causes just mentioned, we can quickly gain an appreciation of their potential complexity:

- For epilepsy and schizophrenia, heart disease and cancer, there are many fields of engagement, including treatment, research, education and training, public information, care, family contacts, campaigning.

- The protection of children includes direct care, intervention before or during crises, family counselling, the provision of helplines; it also reaches out into the raising of public conscience and consciousness about issues of child abuse and work with professionals outside the social work sphere, such as teachers, police, judges and barristers.

- Environmental issues have to do with species, habitats, sustainability, but are not in reality isolated from issues relating to poverty, population growth, health, conflict, the regional or local culture and economy, the activities of the World Bank and the World Health Organisation.

- Functions relating to the health of the people of Whitechapel are divided within and between a wide range of different hospitals and units. They cover the full range of activities just mentioned. There may be special access issues affecting people from minority communities, relating to language, culture and diet as well as health. In any case, there may be local, regional, national or international ramifications to the work.

- The spirituality of its people does seem a clear responsibility for the parish, depending on its churchmanship (for example, high or evangelical) and tradition. Here, too, there are complications, for example with education, schools, secular counselling, music with choir and organ, and the preservation of ancient buildings.

- The provision of opera or other major cultural entertainment seems a clear if complicated matter, including touring and education. However, in relation to plans, and planning, are the Royal Opera House, the ENO, Glyndebourne in the same or adjoining fields? And how do Welsh National Opera, Scottish Opera, Opera North relate to them? What of Opera for All? Or D'Oyly Carte?

- Sports facilities – a major club, a regional centre, a specialised unit, for example for Real Tennis – have roles relating to excellence in an activity, education, recreation, and a focus for mass loyalties. They must take into account the needs of people with physical and mental impairments. They may also be on the border between not-for-profit and for-profit activities, with different activities falling either side of a somewhat wobbly line.

- A great national art gallery is a public resource. It is an archive. It is an educational resource; it may even be a teaching institution, as in the Royal Academy schools. It can also provide commercial services and undertake trading activities, including licensing. Similarly, a small gallery may have all of these roles as well as serving a specialised sector (tanks, lace, decorative design) or functioning as a community resource.

- All universities perform a complex range of functions. Oxford and Cambridge are almost too complicated to include in this series of thumbnail comments. Apart from their obvious functions, they are also internationally recognised historic centres of excellence, with which many people want to be associated. They contain ancient colleges and institutions like the Cavendish, the Ashmolean and FitzWilliam and the Pepys and Bodleian libraries. The colleges, the departments and the universities have significant commercial earning capacities and performance, which is insufficient to meet present or foreseeable needs. Most undertake their own fundraising.

■ A new university, such as the new University for Lincolnshire, may meet a need seen clearly by the CBI, the TEC (now the Learning and Skills Council) and local government. Its establishment showed it was a resource needed within the county but left open the detail of what it would offer, to whom, where and when. Beyond this, the University contributes to the commercial, cultural, sporting and social life of City and County. It is also a national institution.

This arbitrary selection of different types of cause has been cited here to show that it can be difficult to define a cause or field of activity precisely. Such difficulty must be overcome: a cause or field has to be stated and priorities set for activities within and juxtaposed to it. Judgements and choices are involved, which must to some extent be arbitrary. Within the strategic planning exercise, the point is to attack the issues with open and unprejudiced minds and processes.

Issues relating to the cause or field do not end there. The government, media, opinion formers, funding decision-makers and the general public have very different levels of awareness and understanding of causes, and different attitudes and prejudices regarding them. These differences in levels of awareness and understanding will affect provision, communication, public support and therefore fundraising. For example, in the medical field, heart disease and cancer can attract substantial support, perhaps because of their high incidence and the widespread fear in which they are held by the public. By contrast, epilepsy and schizophrenia attract relatively little support, although they too are feared. Indeed, epilepsy is given much lower public provision than diabetes, although its incidence is much higher. Children and animals always receive greater unconsidered support than mental health, the rehabilitation of addicts, and the treatment of abusers. The environment is relatively popular, but priorities in this field may be poorly understood, and environmental behaviour within rich countries of the North (like the UK) does not match the needs or idealism of the cause. How credible are we when we urge good behaviour from the South? Oxford and Cambridge are famous places delivering excellent work across a range of fields: the great or rich can create enduring monuments there or fund research and teaching of the highest value. They both have large numbers of alumni, many great and successful, who will support University as well as College. The companies and individuals whose support created the University of Lincolnshire knew what they wanted to achieve. There are very different situations for other Universities, and some less well-known departments may have few rich alumni and no given constituency of supporters. The great Open University is one example of an innovative, high-achieving centre of excellence – the greatest achievement of Harold Wilson's government – which attracts support only with difficulty.

The starting point of an organisation's strategic plan, therefore, is to determine the following:

- its cause;
- the field or fields in which it operates, and their relative importance;
- public or sectional awareness, understanding of and attitudes to the cause.

Evidence from other organisations in the field

There are larger worlds to be taken into account within which causes and fields must be placed. Analysis depends partly on the establishment of facts and partly, with much greater uncertainty, on qualitative judgements of existing and forecast situations. The closest world to be analysed consists of other not-for-profit organisations of all kinds. In developing a strategic plan, the important considerations are the factors and situations that affect them specifically, and the impact that these have on their fundraising.

Some of these factors are relatively clear, such as the constraints and opportunities given by tax regimes and government regulations for not-for-profit organisations and for supporters. There are specific regulations for this sector concerning, among other things, the ways accounts are prepared, disclosure to the Charity Commission, the responsibilities of trustees and the ways fundraising may be conducted. As this book is prepared, changes to regulations are expected. Less clearly, reports on the state of charities and fundraising in the UK emerge regularly from the umbrella organisations, think tanks and government and occasionally from studies by universities and other institutions. Such information is useful although there needs to be subtlety in the way in which it is applied to any particular strategic decision or decision process, where the aims may be to show this organisation to be exceptional. The kind of information considered here suggests but does not define a context. It seldom reflects the situations within intense appeals, where realities are changed, or in communities (like mine) where giving is part of the culture.

The political context

The UK government seems unlikely in the predictable future to change for the worse the regulatory and tax regimes that are very favourable to not-for-profit activity in the UK. There cannot be the same confidence assessing future EU regulation, particularly if we join the Euro, losing control over our fiscal and welfare policies. The Anglo-Saxon tradition (in the USA, Australia, New Zealand, South Africa as well as the UK) has encouraged a vigorous, independent non-governmental sector – what could be seen as part of the essence of a civil society – which may operate outside the scope of statutory activity and may be critical of it. However, there is a different tradition in Europe, based on an eighteenth-century view of society, fostered by Rousseau among others, that there should be no independent institutions within the state. This has tended to make not-for-profit activity subservient to governments. If future pan-European regulation were based on this doctrine, it would have grave consequences in the UK.

REPRISE

The discussion above has broadened the focus, in order to consider a range of external influences and demands that are part of any organisation's strategic considerations. It is time to narrow the focus again.

In developing a fundraising strategic plan, it must be assumed that two matters have been clarified:

- the cause and field in which an organisation operates, and public awareness and understanding of and attitudes to them;
- the more general context in which not-for-profit organisations are operating, and the contextual factors that affect them.

In the face of these external factors, the discussion must now focus on the organisation itself, and its possible options.

Starting points for strategic planning: in summary

The development of a strategic plan starts with questions like this:

- What are the needs and priorities of our cause and the fields in which we operate?
- What is our organisation's role in relation to them?
- What other provision is there for the needs, from statutory and voluntary sources, and what gaps are there in this provision?
- What is the competition, and how good is it?

- Regardless of current skills, resources and funding, what services should we ideally provide? (Only later will questions progress to: what could we provide?)

The answers to these questions should start from the original objects of the organisation and may in turn question its policies and practice.

Organisations do not want to spend their time permanently on the brink of revolution. Resultant anxiety could paralyse action. However, with not-for-profit organisations especially, which are concerned with constructive idealism, there should be a radical reappraisal when the situation and the context for activity have changed.

This is difficult where a founder (perhaps) and trustees (frequently) either do not want to be troubled by change or lack energy to undertake it. Nevertheless, the questions viewed above raise a series of issues that must be resolved, regardless of what any subsequent planning processes may show to be practicable and affordable, if the plan is truly to reflect the needs in society and challenge existing and potential supporters.

In summary, a strategic plan must resolve these questions:

- Given our objects and policies, our cause and fields of activity, the public's attitudes towards them, the needs and priorities between them, the scope and quality of provision from all sources – what should be the nature, scale and distribution of our services in future, regardless of the resources that we might attain?

- Will this entail changes in our policies and practice? Even in our constitution or charitable objects?

- What are the scale and timings for service delivery?

- What implications are there for capital and revenue expenditures? And for the fundraising targets to meet them?

- What are our renewed vision and mission? How will these be communicated and shared throughout the organisation? Later, they must be shared and communicated outwards.

Strategic planning: internal factors

The previous section was concerned with the ideal, the conceptually desirable. The next stage in the planning cycle involves confrontation of the organisation with its ideal, so that it can consider what it ought to be.

Reviewing an organisation's service provision

Given reaffirmed objects and reaffirmed or perhaps revised policies, it must be established to what extent the forms, scope and quality of the organisation's services currently match that vision and mission; and it must be seen whether present funding performance can support the services needed. It must also be considered whether this organisation can now endure the change that the planning process might require of it.

It is with funding and fundraising that this book is primarily concerned, but funding and fundraising relate to service provision and are justified by it. Fundraisers and volunteer leaders must be satisfied that their activity is for a valued cause and that without it the cause will falter or fail. The review of services – whether these are academic, artistic or relate to health, welfare or poverty – will consider the needs, and the present provision against them from this organisation and other providers, who may be not-for-profit, statutory or for-profit. In many sectors now, commercial and not-for-profit agencies are in competition with each other. Once it has been decided what services ought to be provided, the organisation will be assessed in terms of its current skills, the quality of its operations, and the forms and distribution of services. Should a new course or gallery be added? Should the network of services be extended? Could more effective use be made of IT? These decisions will have implications in terms of revenue and possibly of capital expenditures. At this stage of the planning cycle, expenditures should be calculated to match the *ideal* provision, not what history or timidity suggest. The moment for fiscal realism comes later, after the fundraising appraisal has been made.

It may be that a bold reinforcement of services will carry the organisation to a new level, making it a more attractive object for funding. However, the appraisal of services must be carried through honestly recognising the positive aspects, limits, weaknesses and gaps in the organisation's provision. This appraisal must involve trustees and senior management. It is not a function to be carried out in isolation by fundraising staff. There can be quite radical conclusions on the ways services are planned and delivered. What is ideally desirable for services to match the needs may be unattainable by one agency alone. Two recent, massive programmes were mounted in association or partnership with other agencies, in one case co-operating with organisations from a single field, in the other with organisations from diverse, complementary fields.

Appraising an organisation's funding performance

When it turns to funding, the organisation's first question must be whether current funding performance meets the requirements: whether the intention is to leap forward, edge forward or stand still. It is rare that additional funds are not needed – and at greatly enhanced levels, if a bold plan is to be adopted. The review of funding starts where the organisation is or has been, with the following principal areas for investigation:

Current and former sources of funding of all kinds, including statutory, voluntary, trading and commercial funders, as well as trading and contractual partners. The sources need to be categorised by type and listed, with a record of cumulative income from each over, say, a five-year period. Any special features of relations with main categories of funders or individual funders would be noted.

The routes and methods through which funds have been secured, including fundraising techniques, commercial negotiation, trading, and relations with government departments. This part of the exercise would also consider the people, functions and processes through which some main sources were reached and, perhaps, persuaded.

The investment made in each source or type of source and in the various techniques for reaching them. Without judgement yet about this, the productivity of sources and methods should be appraised. This might involve calculating fundraising income against its direct costs and an apportionment of overheads.

Structures and procedures for maintaining relations with all types of source. The most basic point here is whether there are accurate, up-to-date records of past patterns and sources of support. These should ideally be stored so that they can be analysed statistically and segmented by type, levels of performance, location and other factors that may be useful. The system should hold a full history of the relationships with supporters, and, if it does not, this too is part of the appraisal. Finally, the ways in which relations have been maintained and fostered must be considered.

A key question which emerges from these enquiries is whether the organisation is realising the potential of the sources which support it. Lists often emerge at this point with a high proportion of names significant for fundraising, few or none of them contributing anywhere near their potential or what other organisations have secured from them. Other questions are whether the organisation is covering the full range of sources in principle available to it; and whether the techniques it is using are the most productive available, source by source. For example, is the direct marketing aiming too low in the targets proposed, and is it being aimed at sources that would be more productively reached through other methods? Does the organisation reach major prospects in person or only through their protective shields of committees and grants executives? If the organisation has a regional network, does it reach all levels and types of source from place to place? This stage of the planning cycle involves analysing the range of available sources and the fundraising techniques that could be used to reach and persuade them, while relating costs to likely yields over a sensible time span.

There are special considerations affecting the outcome of this appraisal. For example, there may be sources or techniques that are precluded by the organisation's field of activity, or by its ethos. Tobacco and alcohol companies are often regarded as unsuitable supporters for children's causes; charities are from time to time criticised for dealing with companies that associate with certain governments; gambling-related fundraising is eschewed by Quakers and Methodists. These are constraints. Against these, there are opportunities. For example, it often happens that an organisation that has been ineffective in its attempts to reach main national sources and decision makers has networks for contacts available to it among trustees, alumni, users, visitors, people in the region or neighbourhood, friends, and past and present supporters. The organisations that use these networks can prosper through them.

Assessing the quality of key personnel

There are also questions concerning the positive qualities and the deficiencies of the board or trustees, staff and others, such as volunteers, associated with the organisation. Major fundraising does not and cannot work without the vigilant but complete support of the board and trustees, together with their senior management. Yet this often poses serious problems for fundraising. Few members of not-for-profit boards are selected because of their knowledge and skills in communications, marketing or fundraising. They are more likely, quite legitimately, to have been selected for their academic or artistic standing, or their expertise in areas of treatment, welfare or care. This may equip them for the first part of the enquiry but not for this part, which deals with fundraising and other forms of promotion.

There may be a token marketing person on the board; there is more likely to be a marketing or fundraising sub-group. Frequently, but by no means always, board members and staff remain suspicious of the marketing and money cultures thus represented. This can become a major factor in planning, for example where a respected senior member of the board becomes frightened of development ('let us throw out the computers and concentrate on the poor') or suspicious of the new people introduced to fund it ('they are only here for what they can get out of it'). Business people may change when they join a charity board – for example, in their attitudes to risk and to returns on investment. Whoever undertakes this part of the study – an individual or group – has to make very difficult judgements concerning board and other such figures, and often concerning the senior management as well.

The next series of judgements is equally sensitive. If there are questions about current fundraising performance or the introduction of new target segments of prospects and of refurbished or novel techniques, the skills and quality of existing fundraising management and staff are crucial. These may be adequate; or it may be that, by training existing personnel and introducing one or two new staff, the organisation could deliver the results needed. This is, however, more difficult than it sounds. Familiar people and procedures are often entrenched and nervously defended, and sometimes it will be necessary to introduce, immediately or gradually, an enlarged, reorganised, multi-faceted department, with new staff in the majority. There are big challenges for management here.

There are two certainties around these issues:

- No ambitious programme will succeed unless it is backed by the will and commitment of the board, trustees and senior management.
- Fundraising succeeds, given that backing, where staff and key volunteers have the knowledge, skills, motivation, structures and backing to achieve challenging, attainable goals. 'Backing' here includes investment and all support resources.

This discussion implies a series of methods for measuring personnel and funding performance, against agreed guidelines and targets, for board, trustees and funding volunteers, as well as for the fundraising or development staff. How, about whom, and for whom is fundraising performance measured and reported? Can all or crucial parts of the organisation endure the impacts of a major appeal? This touches people, structures and procedures.

SUMMARY

These enquiries can lead to a new series of decisions, or at least to new options for choice. These principally concern:

- The organisation's desirable objects and the actions needed to achieve them over the next few years, in terms of service, fabric, plant, distribution.

- The context for service delivery, and the competition.
- The funding objects and targets relating to revenue and capital, with their timescale.
- Given their relations with the organisation and their attitudes to it, the ability and willingness of current supporters to meet all or part of the funding targets.
- The new sources to be identified, located, characterised and evaluated through prospect research.
- The fundraising methods to realise this potential from former, existing and new sources of support.
- The critical path and timetable for this (see page 57).
- The design of alternative strategies to achieve the same ends.
- The staff and volunteers required to deliver the funding programme, allowing for recruitment and for training.
- The organisational structures and management procedures.
- The investment required to achieve this and the timing of the net outflow of funds.
- The period over which returns on investment should be seen, and their scale.

Having decided where it wants to go, the organisation should now establish the operational plan for getting there.

It is worth reiterating one less tangible factor to be considered before action may confidently be taken: the will of the trustees, board and senior management to succeed. It is not enough that they make the investment and take a measured risk. A majority at least must be committed to the programme undertaken, putting their trust and enthusiasm into it and, ideally, contributing to it financially at whatever level they could generously afford (something that would be taken for granted in the USA). Fundraising is not a function apart from the organisation: it must form a unity with the organisation's vision, mission and operations.

CHAPTER THREE

The planning process and the strategic plan

There has to be a process to deliver the plan. This will entail private investigation and formal research. The plan itself must be adaptable, depending on the organisation; but it will be expected to cover such points as the vision and mission, the targets, segmentation of funding prospects, methodologies, timetables, resources and investment. They will also consider consolidation of relations with supporters for the future.

Process management

The precise ways in which the planning process is carried through will vary depending on the size and type of the organisation involved. Here again, though, there are principles that apply to any organisation which undertakes strategic planning.

Someone needs to be in charge of the processes of a study, to drive and co-ordinate them. In a small organisation this may be the director. In a large organisation the directorate must be intensely involved, but direction of the processes may be delegated to a senior executive. Indeed, there may be separate directors of the processes: for example, one for the service, teaching and creative functions, and another for the funding development. The processes still need to be driven and co-ordinated. Regardless of an organisation's size, strategic planning may also be put in the hands of an external consultancy skilled in this activity.

In small organisations, the director may form a planning team consisting of senior members of the directorate or of main function heads, perhaps with one or two trustees or other non-staff members. In large organisations there may be a main planning group, or one for funding development and another for services. There may also be individuals or project groups to concentrate on specialised aspects of the study. Organisations of all kinds may also employ consultants to conduct or help with the study.

Whatever the size of the organisation and scale of the exercises entailed, there will need to be a critical path tracking the necessary flow and interactions between all aspects of the study, some of which will be mutually dependent. There cannot be budgeting for costs or targeting for fundraising until capital and revenue activity have been agreed. And until the style of the organisation, the types and scope of its services and the people to be served are known, there cannot be a case for support, or broad segmentation of funding prospects. Related to the critical path there must be a timetable for the study, giving dates for the completion of its various aspects and stages. The timetable should show a programme of meetings (for example between the project leader and the director) for the planning team and for the trustees. It should set dates for reports and for recommendations to the directorate and trustees. It should specify the date the planning process should end and the timings to be followed by directorate and trustees in their tasks for reaching decisions based on the plan's proposals.

Outside comment may be injected into these processes, whether or not consultants are used. Such outside involvement broadens observation and reduces subjectivity. That need not presuppose an open planning process. For some organisations – where the issues are radical and disturbing both to staff and to those served, and carry major implications for the organisation's competitiveness – the planning process may be closed and treated with strict internal and external confidentiality. In a case of this kind, staff and outsiders would be informed and engaged only where necessary and then on the strict understanding that information received and given was to be treated in confidence. As we have seen, this means that the plan for the study will have to resolve when and how staff and volunteers are to be informed, and to what purpose, once crucial strategic decisions have been made.

Research and information

The previous chapter outlined the typical subject matter and outcomes of a strategic study: these concerned the field and cause, an organisation's achieved and desirable roles in relation to them, the related costs and funding targets, the sources of funds and methods of fundraising to achieve these targets, organisational and operational implications and the investment entailed within a medium and long-term time span. On these factors the funding strategy and plan would be based.

The topics in this chapter concern the ways in which the information to underpin decision and action can be gathered, offered and used. There are many distinctions to be made concerning the nature and quality of information used in decision-making. This information can be:

- factual or historical, based on records and reliable recall;
- quantitative, based on data which carry, within statistical limits, probable measures of facts;
- qualitative, based on data which carry no statistical probability but which can provide selective, useful glimpses into minds and behaviour;
- predictive, extrapolating from known facts and stated probabilities to more or less likely futures.

Internal research: key people

At the start of a planning study certain choices have to be made, regardless of the size and type of organisation. There will be key people within and close to the organisation whose knowledge and attitudes must be known and allowed for if there is to be progress. There need to be private interviews with these people to explore their attitudes regarding the organisation, their ambitions for it, and perhaps for themselves as well. Before these interviews begin, it should be made clear that they will be privileged, in the sense that information from them will be recorded and used but not attributed. Such interviews should take an hour at the most and could take much less if, for example, all that is involved is establishing fairly simple facts or opinions. If the planning process is conducted by an employee or outside agency there will almost certainly need to be a series of interviews or briefings with the director, development direc-tor and other key people. Within any organisation there will be some people whose views are essential to the planning study, and there may be others whose views are less significant but whose vanities should not be dented. Interviews can be used as a means of including someone in the process.

A detailed study of this kind, with delivery of the report and recom-mendations on strategy, can usually be completed within eight to ten weeks from commissioning. Two to three weeks before the report is delivered, there may be a verbal report to selected members of the organisation, to test the accuracy and comprehensiveness of the findings and also reactions to the main observations and proposals. Following this verbal report, investigations and the report will be completed.

However, that simple procedure and short timescale will not be appropriate for every fundraising activity and every organisation. A massive appeal for a large and complex organisation will require more multi-faceted processes, with a great diversity of contacts and of interviews for them. In such an appeal, involving prospects or opinion-formers in the planning can be a way of engaging them in the consequent programme. Studies of this kind, involving a large number of investigators and contacts, may take many months, although a planning process which is over-prolonged can induce frustration, boredom and disaffection – and may also suffer from leaks.

Internal research: key documents

There may be records and documents stating the organisation's current situation and aims, proposing future options, declaring or proposing developments. Staff or outside agencies must be given the fullest access to such information. There will be issues of confidentiality with these documents, but the staff and consultants must be trusted to maintain their professionalism and not betray confidences.

Documents that may be relevant here include main discussion or policy papers, the corporate or business plan, if such exists, other public or private statements, as well as full accounts and financial projections.

Key supporters, users and beneficiaries

Great sensitivity is called for when contacting supporters or, more acutely in some categories, beneficiaries, clients and users. There are different issues relating to the two groups. Any private contact with supporters at this stage will be designed to investigate their knowledge, understanding and attitudes relating to an organisation they may have supported in the past with great or minimal personal commitment (people give support out of passion, but also out of fashion). If there are to be individual interviews with supporters as part of the planning process, they must be selective and they must have a clear purpose. Such research can change attitudes and behaviour: it carries some content of information and even of opinion. The interview must therefore be clearly presented as a confidential exercise of constructive significance for the cause and for the organisation – not as a solicitation for funds. If these points are clear, the process itself can help development of significant relationships with the people interviewed, some of whom would most likely be key supporters with a well-established association with the organisation. The people conducting the interviews would be senior staff or volunteers, the consultants or combinations of these. (There should of course be measures and records of supporters' productivity. This will be discussed later.)

Just as it is important for a company to know what its customers think of it, it is important that a not-for-profit organisation knows that its services deliver the benefits intended; it is also important that they know what the recipients of their services or grant making think about them. There is a tough but mutually enlightening aspect of this. It is healthy that certain beneficiaries know that they are at least partly dependent on voluntary support – it might also be useful for them to know about its source or sources. Academics and artists, for example, need not be protected from awareness of the means that make all or parts of their activity possible. If the support is not damagingly coercive or oppressive, knowing who the sources are can introduce constructive realism into beneficiaries' attitudes and behaviour and even cause them to co-operate in fundraising. The situation is totally different where the people receiving services or support are necessarily vulnerable: the poor or the mentally or physically disadvantaged, for example, should not be humiliated or be made to feel they are locked into dependence by the support they receive. With some such people, because of language, culture or condition, it may be impossible to gather information through direct enquiry.

Qualitative research

The previous section suggested private, privileged interviews for key or exemplary individuals. The individual interview works very differently from a small group meeting, where those taking part interact and may take postures, dissimulate or become silent. That does not mean that group research (focus groups) is unhelpful. It is a necessary method for some types and levels of investigation. For marketing, it can deliver rich opinion and perceptions on a product, service or on corporate image. (It is riveting to watch a board or marketing team react from behind a two-way mirror or to a video which brings comment from customers directly to them.) The report on such group research, managed by an expert, can be less dramatic but more informative.

Qualitative research can provide similar benefits for not-for-profit organisations, and has been used effectively with actual and possible supporters. It can also be used selectively with certain beneficiaries of voluntary support. The essence of qualitative research is that participants are selected according to a variety of criteria: age, sex, socio-economic status, occupation, location, relation to this not-for-profit organisation or to others, interests or behaviour. Within the group, they respond to pre-designed promptings and questionings managed by a trained expert. Qualitative research can deliver precious insights, but the products of such research cannot be given statistical weight. You cannot conclude '80 per cent of such people think this' because eight out of ten in a group say it – a group will never be representative of a large marketing or fundraising universe. Despite this, qualitative research can be richly enlightening.

Quantitative research

Unlike qualitative research, quantitative research seeks out representative samples of the universes it investigates, aiming for results that carry statistically significant results within a stated range of probabilities. However, quantitative research (or market or opinion research, as it is more commonly known) can never eliminate doubt or risk. This reservation may be even more important where fundraising research is concerned than it is with products. Statement of an 'intention to give' may be even more ephemeral than an 'intention to purchase'. Bias can be built into the research, particularly where questionnaires are designed by untrained amateurs.

The samples of population covered by quantitative research must be of a size that allows for reliable measures across the total of those interviewed and within the most significant sub-samples. This last point is important for most not-for-profit organisations that undertake quantitative research, perhaps to position the organisation within the total children's or wildlife or medical research field, in order to test awareness and perhaps some behaviour and attitudes. The sub-sample on a particular organisation may be too small to permit further, meaningful analysis within it, like establishing the make up of the set of people who knew its name or had given support, in terms of their age, socio-economic status, sex, and location. The number to be analysed must be large enough to reduce the margin of error to an acceptable level, which might mean that the research should catch at least, say, 150 to 200 respondents within the relevant sub-sample.

Questions for research

The kinds of questions that may be covered by research include the following:

- awareness and understanding of the field or cause;

- awareness and understanding of particular organisations, including the direct competition;
- behaviour in relation to organisations in a particular field or dealing with a cause;
- recognition of images and messages;
- response to particular marketing, fundraising, and communications stimuli;
- attitudes and predispositions in relation to a cause, field or particular organisation.

The findings can be of great value in the planning and execution of a fundraising strategy. Indeed, if awareness, attitudes and behaviour are measured before, during and after its implementation has run its course, they can be used as a benchmark for measuring a strategy's effectiveness. But a research finding is not a fundraising result. Research is an aid, not a substitute for judgement, and never completely dispels the fogs of doubt.

There are other forms of research, discussed in detail by other books in this series, including in-depth interviews and, of course, prospect research.

TOPIC SUMMARY **PROSPECT RESEARCH**

The objectives of prospect research are: to identify, locate, characterise and evaluate sources of funding in principle relevant to an appeal, where there are *prima facie* reasons for believing they would be sympathetic to the cause. Prospect research must also identify early possible volunteer leaders for fundraising. This means that the cause or field, the services delivered or proposed and the targets must be matched to the idealism, interests, behaviour, contacts and means of those to be selected as prospects. An established organisation, with established backers of various kinds, may be able to achieve its aims simply by boosting their levels of support; but it is more likely that it will have to find new supporters to achieve its enhanced objectives, perhaps bringing in new generations.

The task of research is not just to identify the people who might respond to an appeal and to see whether their means might enable them to respond at the levels proposed; it is also to seek out the ways these sources could be reached. What are the routes into this company, trust or foundation? Who are the contacts through whom these individuals might be involved?

The sources of information for this research will start with the organisation's records of support and the networks and knowledge of its patrons, presidents, trustees, council and committee members, and special friends. If the organisation lacks such background, it will have to gather more raw information, searching out the people most likely to respond and become engaged early, perhaps through introductions from an MP, member of the Lords or other public figure. Whatever the organisation, it will also need to use information of all kinds – publications, databases, news, word of mouth – to discover new sources. Some of this can be achieved through staff and volunteers, but the use of an external agency may also be needed.

The review of records should analyse the upper levels of support received and scan them for the more promising names and contacts.

Research of the kinds discussed above, professionally mounted, will usually require the services of external agencies and specialists: it tends, therefore, to be expensive. As a result, an organisation might seek to establish simple facts from its supporters by issuing them with its own questionnaire. There is a caution here: flaws in amateur questionnaire design are common and can compromise the results, so it is worthwhile at least to seek informed expert opinion and to run a small test before the exercise is irrevocably committed.

Because professional research is expensive, its anticipated benefits must be proportionate to its costs. The costs vary depending on the ways research is undertaken. Commissioning a tailor-made, quantitative survey can be very costly. It may be possible to get information which is equivalently useful by having questions asked through one of the general purpose omnibus surveys run by one of the major research companies, or by undertaking research collaboratively with other appropriate organisations.

The strategic plan

Particularly with larger organisations, a range of consultants may be involved in the planning process, for the development of corporate policy and communications as well as fundraising strategies. Where the strategy is of any complexity, demanding change, advice may be needed on the appraisal, training and recruitment of staff and volunteers, and, ideally, the trustees. The specialists involved in the strategic plan could therefore be drawn from all forms of fundraising and direct marketing, to advertising and PR, to corporate image and style, to personnel. This is not an exhaustive list. The key point is that all such inputs must be co-ordinated and directed to a productive end.

The planning process itself will end with the strategic plan, a document presenting and analysing the findings which, with discussion, concludes with proposals or options for action.

What the plan will not contain are blank cheques. All the risks are still to be taken, although greater light has now been shed on the surrounding landscape and the way ahead. There must be some flexibility around the plan, which will still be provisional in many aspects, offering well-founded hypotheses. The proposed track ahead remains conditional until events show that the course is right: for example, establishing whether leadership can be recruited or whether, when tested, the new messages win assent from the target public. There is also the possibility that external events, such as shifts in government policies and provision or an economic crisis, may change the situation for fundraising. All planning is fallible and vulnerable. Nevertheless, the plan must be judged capable of delivering the results intended, mapping the best available route to the organisation's objective.

Contents of the strategic plan

Most plans of this kind would be expected to cover the following points, although there will be variations depending on the organisation and the particular intentions of the exercise (which may have narrow or comprehensive aims):

Aims and methods There should be a statement of the aims and methods of the plan, with a description of how the material is ordered and organised and a survey of the people and organisations who contributed to it.

Main findings Main findings should be presented and discussed with proposals or recommendations as their conclusion. This is the main text. The full supporting details and tables would usually be given in the appendices or the supporting documents.

Interpretation and discussion of facts The facts and figures on their own, without their context and reference to the dynamics of the organisation itself and its field of operation, are not useful. There must therefore be interpretations and discussions of facts indicating or tending towards conclusions. Of concern here will be the present and anticipated needs in the organisation's broad field of activity, this organisation's current situation and future options, given its objects and origins, and the tasks to be undertaken if its activity is to match its own ideals of service and performance.

Vision It is here that the organisation could start to adumbrate its vision (see page 24). The broad vision may be inspiring, but it is also likely to be imprecise. There must be service goals that emerge from it: options for activity in relation to the people served which transform aims and objectives into programmes of work. The organisation develops its mission from the vision, therefore, embracing options for corporate position and service delivery. For fundraising, prospects' understanding and assent will generally remain abstract and uncommitted until the vision and great ambitions are translated into specific actions which can be seen as relevant to the attainment of the declared aims – even if these practical goals illustrate, rather than fully express, the strategy's objectives.

Estimates of costs This should open the way to projecting first estimates of the capital and revenue costs of the programme options. The distinction between these two heads of costs is not academic: they make very different demands on funding and fundraising and affect the methods to be used. There are sources of funding more appropriate to capital than to revenue requirements, for example, and vice versa. Capital costs should be as comprehensive as possible, covering plant and equipment as well as fabric, and allowing for inflation. Projections should include an anticipated schedule of when costs will fall due. Revenue projections should cover a three- to five-year period: most major potential funders will want to see how after, say, three years, revenue will be covered by earned income, grant aid, the Higher Education Funding Council for England, the Sports Council and other such complementary sources. At this stage projections should comprehend all costs anticipated if the full programmes are undertaken, without prejudice concerning sums likely to be raised. Ignorant prejudgement on this can prevent achievement.

Targets The plan evidently needs to include a fundraising target or targets. This seems simple: total up the projected costs, and there is the target. It seldom works out as easily as that. For one thing, the costs of service can only partially be itemised at the outset; for another, an organisation might be able to spend effectively any sum it could raise (although this is unlikely to be the case beyond a certain point, because an organisation's capacity to deliver services may fall below what the needs require). A fundraising target also marks the priority of an appeal, which is a factor which adds to backers' motivations for giving or becoming involved, provided the case for fundraising is persuasive. Some fundraising targets in the past have been determined by needs; others have been set, somewhat arbitrarily, at a level that could motivate and inspire, against a background of almost unlimited demand. An important point is that the target itself is an element in winning a prospect's support.

TOPIC SUMMARY **TARGETS**

The declaration of a fundraising target is not necessarily based on a conclusive calculation. Funding objectives may be:

- short term, to maintain income;
- medium term, more or less dramatically to uplift it;
- long term, to sustain it;
- to achieve once-off objectives. For example where a building, once built, will generate the income needed to keep going.

Unless there is a calculation that defines the funding objectives, there will have to be a more flexible formula. Thus, with some massive targets, it may be necessary to illustrate shorter horizons of needs, with the clear understanding that, by the time the first horizon has been reached, the next will be in view. For example, in one major appeal, the aim was £250 million; this was the horizon, but specific sub-targets stated at the appeal's start totalled only about £120 million.

Determining the overall target is only the beginning of a targeting process. The fundraising plan will need to specify whether individuals, companies or trusts are being targeted, individuals and organisations with large or small means, familiar or unfamiliar with supporting not-for-profit causes. For direct marketing, this means that specific, challenging sums need to be proposed.

For major support fundraising, the stated sub-targets for unit support must define what is required from the sources targeted. (A 'unit of support', as intended here, comes from a single source or decision maker, may be in a simple block of funds, possibly spread over time, or may be a composite made up from family trust, corporate grant, employee fundraising and sponsorship and joint promotion.)

For example, with a £1 million target, the following units of support might be projected:

Units of support	Range of support (£)
One	200,000
Two	100,000
Five	50,000
Ten	20,000
Fifteen	10,000

The implications of this projection are already that there must be over 100 warm prospects for this segment of the appeal, given the number of approaches likely to fail. Increase that number, and personal coverage of these prospects by major leaders becomes organisationally impossible. Furthermore, rich sources have unequal means, and prospects are conscious of this hierarchy. If x is known to be the richest source, y is unlikely to give at a higher level, unless exceptional factors prevail. This is why results generally taper from the top. For most appeals, there is a finite number of prospects who are in principle available or who in practice can be reached.

Review of sources The plan must review the sources which might in principle respond to this cause and vision at the levels projected. Depending on the organisation's situation and objectives, it may be necessary to look for long-term as well as one-off sources. Indeed, for any strategy of significant complexity there will have to be segmentation of sources of all kinds. The opening situation will vary depending on whether the organisation: has established bodies of supporters; is starting fundraising for the first time; is a brand leader; or is small, specialised, little known and perhaps unpopular. The organisation will need to use prospect research of various kinds to establish who might be the supporters to deliver the sums required, applying criteria that allow for the findings of the planning investigations as well as the funding objectives.

Leadership team The prospect research must also help identify people who might give early leadership in a major support programme. These might be existing supporters or new prospects. What is essential is that leaders should be selected because they match challenging criteria, not because they are easy to reach and perhaps need something to do.

Long-term programmes For organisations with long-term programmes, the plan should consider the systems and procedures needed to establish prospect research as a continuing process.

The right amount of detail The sources identified through prospect research will be of disparate means. For any major support activity, some will have been profiled, and a relatively large amount of information gathered on them. Such detail will evidently not be useful or attainable within a larger universe of support, for example for direct marketing or public fundraising activities. Here prospects may be designated more broadly, in terms of demographics, occupation or profession, location and religion.

Selecting appropriate fundraising methods and techniques For each band of prospective supporters, therefore, fundraising methods are to be selected that are likely to deliver optimal results cost-effectively. Fundraising methods or techniques have limits to their potential, as do the prospects themselves. The techniques available range from peer solicitation by committed supporters, through peer group approaches and personalised solicitations by mail, down to door-to-door visits, fundraising events, street collections and leaflet drops. This means that there must be segmentation of methods as well as of prospects. Many organisations start with a more or less adequate body of supporters. Relations with them and their capabilities change over time, and some will be dropped as being unproductive; but the system and procedures must also allow for upward mobility, as increased support is invited and received.

TOPIC SUMMARY **SEGMENTATION**

A pattern for segmentation might look like this:

Prospect categories	Support band (£)	Methods
Richest individuals	5m–50m	Exclusive peer contact
Rich individuals	100,000–5m	Peer contact and solicitation
Prosperous individuals	100,000–1m	Peer and group contact Personalised mailings
Rich companies	100,000–2m	Peer contact and persuasion at chair, chief executive level Negotiations at marketing director level Promotions
High-earning individuals	5,000–100,000	Peer and group contact Personalised mailings
Medium-sized companies	5,000–100,000	Peer contacts Approach through public affairs or marketing
Institutional trusts		Contact with director Meetings with director and some trustees
General public		Direct marketing, telephoning, e-mail, trading Collections and events

The summary above does not explore the possibilities exhaustively. Where the return will justify this, 'seeing is believing' visits are valid for all prospects. Of course, these sources are not limited to the methods mentioned (see Mullin, 1995 for a fuller treatment): trusts are given one entry only because most are subsumed under the 'Rich' and 'Richest' categories; prospects in all categories will need to be given some indication of the support sought from them, and of when and how this could be given. This segmentation will vary from plan to plan, depending on each organisation's situation.

Communications Communications of many kinds are needed within most funding and fundraising programmes. These communications may be internal or external, directly or indirectly related to fundraising. (See Chapter Four, page 60, which returns to this discussion.)

The case statement A crucial document needs to be prepared as internal agreement is reached and external briefings begin, with the recruitment of leaders. This is the case statement, which must carry assent from within the organisation concerning its future and its needs, following the processes just outlined. The case statement also becomes the basis for engaging key outsiders, whose opinions, endorsement and leadership may be needed during the early phases of the funding programme. The case statement can be used as the basis for letters and briefings and will be subject to change, reflecting progressively the comments and views of the early leadership, who will thereby be making it their own. Eventually the case statement will be used as a basis for briefing writers and agencies retained to develop the programme's brochures and other communications tools. The plan itself will at least set out the logic of the case for support and may also propose a draft text.

TOPIC SUMMARY **THE CASE STATEMENT**

This is a succinct but full statement of the reasons for a funding programme. It will position the cause or field in relation to the broad world of competition and the particular organisation or programme within its own field. The statement, as a result of the planning processes described earlier, will carry internal institutional approval. It will be the first declaration of vision and mission.

However, as well as being a vehicle for reflecting internal assent, the case statement will be a principal instrument for communicating the organisation's strong arguments for support beyond itself. It must therefore be articulated in a way that takes account of people's prejudices, ignorance and misunderstanding about the field or organisation and avoids the jargon and assumptions of the organisation's staff and others within its field.

This statement has many external roles. It will be a potent part of any movement the organisation is to make to mass communication and persuasion, and an important tool for the engagement of early leaders and supporters in a major support programme, or other exercise of this kind. The style and level of argument should be cool and rational. The object is to draw prospects in as partners in the enterprise. Consequently, the case statement they are given at this stage is a draft that they can modify. In this way it becomes their own, not just the organisation's, statement. One way of doing this is to provide prospects with the declaration of a clear, simple, apparently attainable, incomplete but great and revolutionary idea.

Communications strategy The plan must specify or indicate a communications strategy. At its most complicated level this includes: public relations, which must support and not pre-empt or compromise the fundraising; and advertising, which can play a range of tactical roles in relation to the funding programmes, for example, raising awareness or projecting a common message or image. Beyond this, there may be requirements for a variety of presentation aids and for prospectuses and brochures produced to professional standards appropriate to the target audiences and to the cost benefit they may yield. There will also be consideration of the uses of IT for internal and external communications.

Staff and volunteers The fundraising study should also consider a series of desirable issues, prescinding from their attainability: services and their costs, sources of funding in principle available, and routes and techniques for reaching and persuading these sources. Equally, it should consider the capacity of staff and volunteers to deliver the desirable results. The plan must discuss these matters and make recommendations or proposals on what should be done in terms of training, recruitment and motivation of staff and volunteers.

Management and administration There are implications here for the organisation and structuring of staff and volunteers, and for management and administration. These will include reporting and monitoring lines and systems, with their related IT requirements.

Timetabling The critical path and the timetable for the funding programmes are crucial. Much will depend on the size of the organisation and the scale of the enterprise. There are evident dangers in a complex strategy: there must be no triggering of low-level responses through ill-timed publicity; modest propositions must not get in the way of major peer approaches; staff, volunteers and other resources must be deployed to optimum effect. The methods chosen must work together, not against each other. Supporters can be persuaded to deliver multiple, cumulative support in an appeal, but only if the messages and contacts are appropriately organised. This is a matter for the critical timetable, which must be strongly and effectively managed (see Appendix 2, page 143, for one such timetable). On a separate issue, events must be so ordered that activity allows for the fact that one action may be the prerequisite for the success of consequent actions: their sequence must be designed for achievement. This is a matter for the critical path. Vision has led to mission and mission to the operational plan, detailing action.

Remaining in touch with supporters Achievement of one or a series of funding programme objectives opens relations with significant numbers of supporters. The plan should not close them, except in the case of a one-off objective, fully achieved when the targeted sum is delivered. Even in this situation there should be acknowledgement and recognition proportionate to the support given. With most other appeals, this funding programme will be followed by others. Supporters of all kind who have responded must be acknowledged and taken into account. A less routine point also has to be recognised: with some of the people, trusts and institutions that have backed the organisation, there will have been new understanding of its values, which have been shared through the support committed. The supporter has made a declaration, not a gesture, even if this was muted at the time. This offers opportunities for future mutually rewarding partnerships between the organisation and at least a few of its supporters, and the plan should propose structures and procedures for this.

Budget As a conclusion to all these processes, and as a guide to what may be viable, there is the budget. This will set costs of all kinds against projected income of all kinds, allowing for the incidence of both. For a simple programme, this may be straightforward; for a complex programme, there will be various levels of risk, and the plan must allow for this. An elaborate planning process and its conclusions can be traumatic, even for a confident and long-established organisation. The budget and financial controls must be set in ways that do their best to measure the risks and opportunities, while still allowing for decisions, against bold but pragmatic criteria, on whether the programme should or should not be launched or allowed to continue. Such decisions will at first depend on weighted probabilities but will later be focused on points of achievement defined in the critical path and timetable. The strategy can eliminate neither risk nor chance. It can, however, try to accommodate them.

Mission statement All principal people have been touched by this planning process, which should have searched back to the organisation's origins and the ideals from which it has developed. This will have reaffirmed a vision of service which is demanding but shared by those involved thus far. The strategy now points to new horizons for service and to the funding that will allow the organisation to reach and go beyond them. An operational plan, specifying within this strategy the actions to be taken (together with their sequence, timing and a statement of who is responsible for them), shows how the organisation will move from its starting point to the place or places it must reach. The all-embracing statement of what is to be achieved, in fulfilment of the vision, is the mission statement. The organisation's mission declares the destination it has decided it will reach; the strategy details how it will get there.

TOPIC SUMMARY **MISSION STATEMENT**

The organisation's mission statement declares its corporate, service and consequent funding options. The mission is the practical statement of attainable objectives for the realisation of the vision within the strategy. Given the strategy's necessary flexibility, the mission statement is a reference point for decisions on tactics and development of resources. It presents the options and objectives for actions.

Implementing the plan

Bold, vigilant, flexible management is needed for implementation of any strategy which is exposed to chance. For any major fundraising programme, there must be leadership from within the organisation and from informed, active, external allies. Synergy must be created between parts of the strategy, as its momentum grows. Issues here include structures, the critical timetable, communications and aftercare for all key people and institutions involved.

Management

As an organisation starts implementation of the strategy, having decided which service and funding options to adopt, there is its plan to guide it, pristine and whole. Life will now put it to the test and modify it. The plan has not eliminated uncertainty and cannot prevent chance; there are no blank cheques.

Whatever the organisation's situation, management of the strategy must be bold, vigilant and flexible, demonstrating unwavering commitment to its intended outcomes. The director responsible for implementation in a small organisation, or those to whom responsibility for this has been assigned in a large one, must be given the latitude and resources to carry the plan through regardless of vicissitudes. There should be minimal political interference with a commander in the field.

Clearly, there will be no problem if everything happens as scheduled in the plan. If development is slower than expected, however, the reasons for this must be understood, so that plans can be modified and investment adjusted. If development never starts, or if it stops, the programme will have to be aborted, ideally with some gain to the organisation and certainly with the least possible damage. The implications here are two-fold: first, that sound monitoring and reporting systems, combined with a regime that gives due scope to the fundraising, are essential; secondly, that there need to be sufficient skilled staff backed with adequate resources.

It is a problem if the board, trustees and senior management do not understand the main elements in the plan. For example, they may not appreciate the time it takes to build productive direct marketing or the roles and expectations of leaders in a major support programme. Similarly, they may not appreciate the qualities they should look for in the staff who will manage their strategy or the levels of remuneration reasonably expected by staff of the quality required.

As we have seen, different situations will be handled differently in larger and smaller organisations. Similarly, there will obviously be differences depending on the conclusions of the plan. If these are that there should be a boost to existing fundraising, with no major leap forward for this or for the organisation as a whole, the implications may be slight: an increase in investment and publicity, maybe, but no major staff changes. On the other hand, if there is to be a major shift in services with a repositioning of the organisation and a quantum leap upwards in its fundraising, then the implications are huge. Staff, training, investment, existing volunteers and supporters – all may be affected. New funding development teams may have to be introduced and ill-qualified staff replaced. Organisational and management strains must be accommodated.

These are matters which must be faced and dealt with in order to avoid crisis. The board may mostly be made up of environmentalists, academics, artists, social-work or health specialists – in other words, specialists in service provision – and may therefore need to recruit a few members whose backgrounds are relevant to the development programmes. Alternatively, they might delegate executive responsibility for oversight of the programme to a trusted, differently specialised sub-group. This latter course can concentrate the attention and time of busy people where they can be most effective, avoiding the mutual frustrations which arise when very different people are forced to work together intensely for disparate objectives. Even if they are fully competent to oversee the fundraising programmes, the trustees, board or council may want to engage specialists who will help the organisation in its management of change.

Trustees, staff and volunteers must be prepared for the demands of an intense programme before they embark on it. Such a programme requires concentration of resources and, once it has been successfully started, it will build a momentum which becomes relentless. This sounds a desirable situation to be in, with all parts of a programme driving forward, but there are disadvantages too. The

machine may be crashed but it cannot be slowed down without causing the kind of structural damage that will prevent it from reaching
its destination. Withdrawing investment, or suddenly and drastically
reducing it, is one such way of causing damage; another is diverting
key staff and volunteers to other objectives or allowing their concentration to become dissipated.

Total fundraising programme

There is a special type of intense fundraising programme that can be
delivered by an organisation with broad national standing and universal assent to its objects and cause: such fundraising programmes
can therefore be designed to reach a critical mass which will allow
them to deliver increasing returns. There is a moment in such a programme when, given synergy between its parts and phases, most of
its components begin to exceed their targets, with many people and
groups at all levels wanting to join without additional persuasion, if
they are given the opportunity to do so. A decade ago, this was
achieved by the NSPCC and the Great Ormond Street's Wishing Well
appeals. Today Comic Relief achieves it through its Red Nose Day,
and so, on a narrow scale, does the London marathon. It was
attempted through the Telethon. It is possible to design such programmes, but they are appropriate for a limited number of organisations or causes. They also need huge commitment by the
organisation mounting them. National organisations have failed
when, despite wanting the result and creating the plan, they failed to
charge the operation, functionally, with the resources needed or,
morally, with the commitment of their will to succeed.

Any fundraising programme can be damaged by events outside the
organisation's control. An economic downturn may reduce the sums
achievable, if the strategy was designed before the economic crisis
occurred. A company that is making extensive redundancies may
find it difficult to give generously, even if the effect of the redundancies will be an increase in its profitability. A change in the tax regime
may hurt or stimulate one or more segments of possible supporters,
for example the 'prosperous' category. Policies on the care of elderly
people may reduce the sums available for legacies, as houses are
sold and savings spent. An appeal may also be ambushed by events
or by the competition: a national charity in a difficult field was forced
to abort a major appeal because a more popular competitor
launched a similar programme with its leadership already in place.
Third world agencies may even resort to poaching each other's direct

marketing lists. And yet, if the strategy and its management are strong enough, they should survive all but the direst attacks.

Problems, including possible uncontrollable external factors, need as far as possible to be anticipated so that the programme's structures and procedures can deal with them. The structure needs to allow the board and senior management to be able to oversee and direct the activity but also to give those driving the strategy the scope and initiative required. Large and small organisations will have different structures – and some of our larger national institutions have structures of exceptional complexity – but the principles remain valid, whatever the size, nature or complexity of the organisation.

Structure and leadership

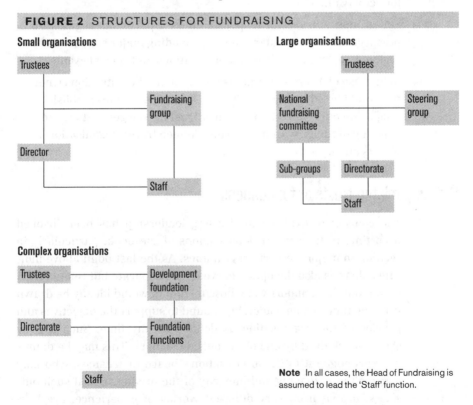

FIGURE 2 STRUCTURES FOR FUNDRAISING

Note In all cases, the Head of Fundraising is assumed to lead the 'Staff' function.

The small organisation may handle its fundraising through a group dedicated to this purpose, probably including the directorate and perhaps one or two trustees, if these have something to contribute.

A large organisation may adopt a more complex structure, including within it any of the following:

- A steering group between the funding programme's main committee and the board or trustees. The steering group might consist of the director, a couple of selected trustees, perhaps an outside leader and the consultant. This might meet on a monthly or six-weekly basis when action is intense, less frequently when it is not.

- A national committee which would represent all main elements in the programme, for example through the people chairing principal groups or sub-groups, such as major support, regions, media, events. This might meet only occasionally or more frequently as determined by the dynamic of the fundraising. The committee's objects might include the exchange of information, creation of synergy and productive competitiveness, and mutual reinforcement for activity and morale.

- Sub-groups with specific responsibilities for particular segments of prospects or for particular projects, including major support and regional appeals as well as communications and special events.

- In the case of a complex organisation and in other situations where this would be advantageous, it may be constructive to establish a separate but related foundation or trust for the generation and handling of funds, within terms determined by the organisation's objects and its policies.

Creating related trusts or foundations

The concept of external fundraising leadership has been invoked from time to time in previous sections of the book, particularly in relation to major support programmes. As the last point above indicates, there is also the option of creating a separate but related trust or foundation, a majority of whose members would ideally be drawn from the fundraising leadership, bound to support the objectives and policies of the organisation as defined at any time. Such a body should be chaired by one of the outside leaders. This may be daunting or repugnant to the organisation's board or trustees, who may fear for the autonomy and integrity of the organisation if such outsiders, drawn from very different worlds of experience, are harnessed to it. Trustees may fear that powerful people, inexperienced in the organisation's field of concern, may ignorantly and damagingly force their views on it. So why propose a course that is so disturbing? The principal intention is to give such major, committed supporters a role and authority of the kind to which they feel, and are, accustomed. It gives them status in this function, and is a reassurance to them. It also gives the organisation a vehicle through which it can maintain active relations with these people and, in due course, replace them.

Certainly care should be taken with the establishment of such a related trust or foundation. Proper controls from the original not-for-profit body must be in place, and the legal aspects will require specialist attention. Supporters' intentions must be protected. It is best that outside members of such a body should not be allowed to serve for more than two consecutive three-year terms. On one of the rare occasions that a trust tried to hijack the organisation it should have served, it was because the trust's relationship with the charity was ill-constituted. In any case, the idea of a related trust is optional and will be appropriate only to certain organisations and situations. The trust or foundation distances voluntary funds raised from the statutory provision of, say, a university, hospital, or other kind of organisation, thus to some extent safeguarding both. Should this option not be appropriate, there are other, usually weaker options, such as the establishment of senior sub-groups to board or council. The aim is to make the organisation more efficient and productive, not to create an unnecessary multiplication of bodies.

TOPIC SUMMARY **FUNDRAISING LEADERSHIP**

For a major support programme, fundraising leaders are people financially committed to the cause at an exemplary level who will use their contacts and personal persuasion to bring in a quota of the higher units of support projected. Such leaders will usually be people who can directly determine, or conclusively influence, decisions on funding at such levels from single sources or combinations of sources: private means, trusts or foundations, and companies. Their active, personal advocacy and persuasion is the strongest method for securing support from prospective supporters with the highest potential in a major support programme. Their involvement does not, however, exempt the organisation's trustees and senior management from their responsibilities for leadership.

Critical path and timetable

The critical path and timetable for any appeal will order activity in relation to its term and, for management of the programme, will define crucial moments in the implementation of strategy: achievement of objectives on time. Delay or failure will call for reappraisal of the action to be taken. It is through the organisational structure and the timetable that the programme managers will make sure that methods and groups reinforce, and do not obstruct, each other. For example, in a strategy which uses a multiplicity of methods to reach a range of target segments for support, it is important that lower-pitched, more popular methods do not interfere with activity in the upper segments designated for major support. However, later, with their major support committed, some of those supporters may be pleased to back the programme again within a short timespan at lower levels; and later at higher levels.

Here is an example of the progression of support from an individual within an appeal (several supporters did this):

£150,000 →   £25,000   →   £5,000
opening gift   exclusive dinner   a privileged seat at a glittering gala

The critical timetable will offer gates for reappraisal and decision to the trustees and steering groups. If one cluster of activity which must precede another has yet to be achieved, should other elements proceed, be delayed or cancelled? If interim achievements are delayed, should the fundraising programme be extended, modified or abandoned?

The critical path will map a course showing what actions are necessarily consequent on others. For example, the case and targets cannot be set until the organisation has determined its capital and revenue programmes; a major support programme should not be launched until the leadership and a number of marker gifts are in place; a massive warm mailing cannot go out until the cold recruitment has been completed. The timetable will set dates for achievements which may be predetermined (the date when building must begin, the period set by a lottery board for securing partnership funds, some anniversary) or may be determined by some other factor: a key person's availability or term of office, a limit to the investment budget, volunteers' morale and patience, the restraint of internal staff and resources. There will also be reporting systems to map progress against both the critical path and timetable, which effectively form a unity. This timetable should, if possible, be drawn up with some generosity, so that the fundraising is not designed to move from crisis to crisis – although sometimes tight scheduling is enforced by circumstance. For as long as activity keeps up with the timetable, all remains positive. It is when achievement is significantly delayed that the monitoring system sounds its alarms. There is also a point at which a fundraising programme will, through entropy, run out of energy and coherence if it becomes over-prolonged, without event. (A model timetable is illustrated in Appendix 2, page 143.)

CHAPTER FOUR **IMPLEMENTING THE PLAN**

The progressive, controlled introduction of fundraising methods is part of a complex strategy, as new segments of prospects become engaged in the programme. There are implications for this in the discussion of programmes just outlined. Such a phased exercise makes big demands on management to maintain the momentum of the overall programme. It may be that some elements will move ahead faster or slower than anticipated, modifying the strategy as originally conceived. This is where skill is needed in managing the strategic plan. Problems can occur if some elements of the plan become over-protracted. For example, when a leadership team meets in a major support exercise it should be to solve problems and report and plot achievement. The leadership team should be composed of busy people who are used to making things happen, so the meetings should not become repetitive, covering the same names and issues month after month. Nor should the process become protracted: often, the more time that is allowed, the sooner chaos enters and entropy takes hold. If this happens, membership and activity will falter or vanish.

It is here that leadership, and prudence, are needed from trustees and staff, as well as external leaders. Leadership is most seriously tested when there is greatest confusion and adversity, which is also the time when trustees, like governments in wartime, may interfere with the leadership's conduct of its campaign; the impulse to charge into the cannons' mouths, regardless of likely destruction, should be resisted, as should the jettisoning of achievement by retreating or cutting loose because of surmountable distress. It is here that a strong, informed leader must be in place who can interpret the immediate situation and judge between the new options, which may be to withdraw forces or to rally them and move them to a positive, conclusive outcome. This is valid for the implementation of fundraising, as it is for military, strategy.

Internal synergy and co-operation

There must be synergy between the separate parts of the more intense programmes, all mutually reinforcing each other. The synergy and co-operation also need to be at work within the organisation itself. People within the not-for-profit sector will be familiar with this issue, even if it seems strange to people outside it. The problem is that the fundraising function is frequently neither understood nor esteemed by those responsible for the not-for-profit organisation's activity. There may even be hostility between the development and service delivery personnel. At its least antagonistic level, the problem may be one of understanding, but experienced fundraisers will be accustomed to the perception of fundraising as simply a mechanical process that depends on slogans and impulsive public responses, rather than on sympathy based on understanding and idealism shared through the gift. Typically in this situation, the fundraisers ask the service providers for details on the services responsive to needs which are planned and on the related budgets. The answer comes back: just tell us what services you can raise the money for, and that's what we'll give you. A response of this kind deems the objectives of fundraising to be frivolous and the supporters of a cause shallow. The point needs to be made again: the value of fundraising's objectives match those of the cause and of the organisation's services; there must be unity between them.

The situation is worse where there is a divide or even hostility between the people responsible for fundraising and those responsible for service delivery. Some time ago, a consultant was asked to find out why a university's development department was not functioning productively. What he found was that the development director had moved his office off campus, where it tried to operate in detachment from the university's life and work. The development director was not qualified for his task and was despised or ignored by the academic staff; in his turn, the director held the academic staff in suspicion.

This problem was overt, but when the antagonisms are covert, the situation can be more difficult to resolve. For example, with an environmental agency where there was a similar rift between fundraising and the wildlife specialists, a major fundraising programme started under suspicion and proceeded with its critics sniping and always ready terminally to attack the programme. It inevitably and unnecessarily failed.

Fundraising cannot magically succeed in such circumstances. It is an organic part of any organisation which depends on its results. This is why it must proceed with the will and active support of board, staff and management. It is difficult for fundraising to succeed if it has staff without management support; or management without staff support.

Communications

Communications of all kinds are needed for implementation of the strategy, among which are the following: alerting, informing, educating, persuading, reporting and motivating all the plan's external target publics, as well as the internal staff and volunteers.

Vehicles for these communications may comprehend the full range, from private meetings and small functions through group briefings, private letters, a prospectus or brochure, videos, promotions to advertising and editorial. There should be a clear objective and target public for each type and form of communication. For example, in a large organisation which undertakes a complex funding programme there may be regular bulletins to keep all staff and volunteers informed, and occasional statements marking key stages in the strategy's progress, as well as special communiqués directed to particular teams or staff groups. The report forms used by management to track what is happening as well as the reports that show the findings are in themselves communications tools. In the large organisation, responsibility for communications may be split between public affairs or public relations and fundraising. The primary role of a bulletin, statement, publication or event is usually obvious, so that it can be seen whether it has to do with communications and corporate affairs generally or specifically with fundraising. The demarcation of responsibilities will be less of an issue in a smaller organisation but, whether the organisation is large or small, communications with staff, volunteers and main categories of supporters must be planned, not taken for granted. Osmosis is not an effective way to transmit information and messages.

Fundraising entails persuasive communication. Someone who has already supported the organisation must be persuaded to increase support, in terms of scale and perhaps frequency; someone who has not yet supported the organisation must be persuaded to do so (in this instance, the communication may take longer). The first requirement of all communication is the same, regardless of the segment of potential support being considered: to understand the awareness, knowledge, attitudes, means and relevant behaviour of the people to be approached. All good communication starts from insight into the minds of the target prospects and empathy with them. It then finds the best, most cost-effective ways to reach them; frames the argument – allowing for their knowledge, understanding and prejudices – most likely to convince them; carries the a-rational charge which may motivate them (this may be emotional or, for example, social if they are being invited to join a peer group or move up into a desired social group); and reaches a conclusion aimed at some specific response – to ask for more information, to come to dinner or attend a function, to give at the suggested level. Selection of the form of communication becomes part of the communication itself: the quality of materials, the style of the function, the media used.

TOPIC SUMMARY **PERSUASIVE COMMUNICATION**

This is an eloquent statement, taken from *Ratio docendi & discendi* (1702) by Père Jouvancy SJ (whose outstanding pupil was Voltaire), of the Jesuit principle that you go in through someone's door and bring him out through yours:

In choosing arguments, one must above all take account of those which affect the listener and are appropriate to his opinions, his mind, his condition and his age. We are all attracted by the true or false appearances of that which is good, but what is good for me is not so for you. This thing may be useful to that person; this other thing may be pleasing and honourable for these people, while in different circumstances something else pleases and delights us. As men will only let themselves be led by reasoning that accords with their feelings, this means that in addition to evidence that enlightens our minds, we must excite the passions, if the subject permits it, to undermine the will. To this end, it would be most useful to know the manners of men and the nature of movements of the soul. For every kind of cause, one must excite different passions.

A mass appeal's communications will usually be based on fairly broad generalisations about its target prospects. Refinements can be introduced as segments of prospects are narrowed, allowing for more precise information about attitudes, lifestyles and behaviour. At the other extreme, a major support programme will use detailed profiling and networking, with the case being presented as a common brief but where the individual messages and the ways these are delivered will be designed with a specific individual, corporation, trust or foundation in mind.

In management of the strategic plan, due time and resources must be allowed for the research demanded by good communications, or there will be wastage of effort. There must also be a guarantee that there are the right skills for the job. For example, copywriters with high skills for large-scale direct marketing in preparing the prospectus for a major support exercise may not be able to find the style, tone of voice or emphasis needed to engage high level prospects, who may respond better to the style of the *Financial Times* than to *Reader's Digest*. Exaggeration in statement or emotion, and the swiftly made proposition, are not appropriate here.

Consolidation of relations

There are very few organisations who will no longer need the people and institutions that supported it once the fundraising strategy has run its course, even if there was a finite, one-off object for a funding programme – the completion of a building project, purchase of equipment, funding of an event or a games. There will almost always be valuable contacts and relations to be passed on to some other, later endeavour. For most organisations the strategic plan that has just been achieved will lead through to others into an indefinite future. The gains from implementation of this plan must be consolidated so that the next plan starts with added advantage in terms of the organisation's service delivery, its competence for service and, for our purposes, its constituencies of committed supporters and its skills and resources for funding development. These are gains on which the future can be built, if they are deliberately and systematically consolidated.

There are many ways in which support and contacts can be consolidated and graded according to the levels of support received and the organisation's expectations of the supporters involved. The starting point here is the fact that the satisfactions in support for a not-for-profit cause are mutual and include the person or institution providing the funds. This may be their only way to share in your ideals and service – and satisfaction is greater the more generous the support provided. Everybody likes to be personally acknowledged, if only by a postcard from the chairman or director. This basic acknowledgement may in itself generate increased future support.

However, most people would like to know what the organisation is doing with its money. Annual reports or bulletins can meet this need, but people may feel more involved if there is an interesting, informative publication addressed to them. Some supporters may want special information covering a particular field of activity. There may be categories of membership, partnership, friendship associated with receipt of such information. Time is also part of the investment, again depending on levels of support and anticipated returns. Some staff and volunteers within the organisations may be personally assigned to cultivate relations with particular main supporters; there may even be a department responsible for this. Receptions for supporters can be productive in terms of information shared, contact and support. For higher-level prospects, there may be 'seeing is believing' visits to an organisation's projects, in the UK or overseas, to make its abstract claims real. Arts and academic organisations have special opportunities. Most high level funders of the arts enjoy privileged access to events and meetings with principal figures from the arts world. They may also be given flattering recognition. Busy business people can appreciate contacts with academics and may enjoy the high table or a close briefing on new developments. All such supporters might be eligible for special recognition as Presidents, Patrons, Funding Partners or as honorary Fellows, Masters, Doctors. Oxford has even invented a special gown and ceremony for its benefactors, cleverly avoiding academic conflict. These are matters for sensitive but pragmatic decision in managing the last stages of strategic implementation: looking to the future.

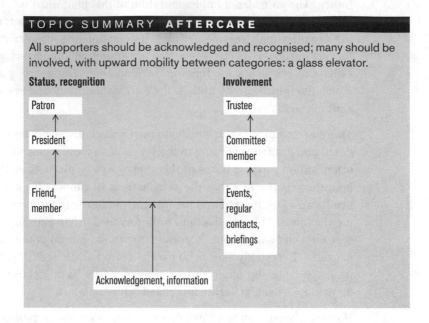

TOPIC SUMMARY **AFTERCARE**

All supporters should be acknowledged and recognised; many should be involved, with upward mobility between categories: a glass elevator.

Status, recognition

- Patron
- President
- Friend, member

Involvement

- Trustee
- Committee member
- Events, regular contacts, briefings

Acknowledgement, information

The design and implementation of strategies are for most organisations part of a continuing process – with one horizon achieved, another is to be attempted – which is also a process of continual renewal.

As the funding processes progress and succeed each other, the organisation grows in understanding of itself and of its supporters. Its best staff will become managers of this knowledge. Through it, the organisation and its relations with supporters will develop. With strategies which are dynamic not static, the organisation will in a true sense function as a learning organisation.

As valued supporters and fundraising partners move forward with you, they grow older; new generations of supporters and partners must be recruited and engaged. Periodically, deliberate effort should be made to bring in new, younger generations. For example, for major support, there might be special emphasis in the research to identify new prospects under the age of 55 who had the means, contacts, influence and predisposition to join the programme's leadership, or at least to support it at a high level. More might be done through communities, including a company's employees. There are generous idealists in every socio-economic category and age group, some of whom have just reached the point where they want to have an impact on society beyond their direct area of achievement. In a current major appeal, two of the leading, multi-million-pound gifts have been from new wealth, with donors under 40 years old. The fundraising cycle shown below works as the basic form and discipline for planning because fundraising strategy for most organisations is a continuous, developing process: as one cycle ends, it feeds and boosts the next.

TOPIC SUMMARY **THE FUNDRAISING CYCLE**

The cycle is a basic fundraising discipline which has proved valid for any type of fundraising – spectacular disaster appeals being an exception. It has been applied successfully to local, regional, national and international campaigns, and has four cardinal points:

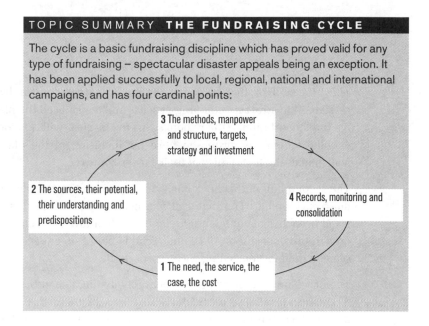

3 The methods, manpower and structure, targets, strategy and investment

2 The sources, their potential, their understanding and predispositions

4 Records, monitoring and consolidation

1 The need, the service, the case, the cost

Interlude

The first half of this book has defined strategy for fundraising, reviewed the strategic planning process and considered the plan and its implementation. Other books in the series will explore the detailed techniques proposed here for inclusion in the plan. This book places the techniques in their larger context.

The second half of this book consists of case studies that are, for the most part, veiled. The material has been dealt with in this way to avoid breaches of confidentiality and also to allow for greater frankness in the exposition. All the material is based on experience. This seemed the most enriching way to present it.

The preceding chapters have repeatedly distinguished between different organisations, particularly in terms of their size. This is a basic differentiating factor between them. A greater range of distinctions or types is now going to be applied. This is not the order in which they will be described, but hierarchically they can be set out thus:

- National and international, well-known organisations, working for causes which carry wide assent, hence with almost universal appeal.
- National and international, well-known organisations with specialist but still broad appeal.
- Great national institutions with a determined constituency or narrow focus.
- Medium-sized organisations with the potential to grow to national or international status.
- Medium-sized organisations with a narrow focus, perhaps dealing with an unpopular or unfashionable cause.
- Organisations with mainly regional impact.
- Organisations with mainly local impact.

- Exceptional organisations and causes
- One-off fundraising objects.

There are overlaps between these categories, which are themselves not comprehensive and are certainly arbitrary. Other factors which will be introduced include religion and fields of activity such as education, health and the arts. The main point here is to recognise the obvious fact that there are significant differences between organisations apart from differences of size.

As different organisations undertake their strategic planning exercises, so they will have different intentions and expectations. These may be: to sustain or improve services; to sustain or increase income and market share; to re-position the organisation; to initiate a crusade for a great cause. Or the aims may be more banal, however rich the opportunities: to mark the organisation's anniversary; to take part in a Year of Something; and so on.

Before moving into what must be some very busy description and discussion, a number of cardinal points need to be revisited. For any organisation, strategic planning should clarify:

- Objects, responsibilities, scope and limits for service and action.
- Options for future policy, service, objectives and action.
- Implications for capital and revenue costs.
- Anticipated income and its reliability if no new initiative were taken.
- Assessment of the potential for new and continuing sources funding.
- Options for harnessing this potential: methods, critical path and time restraints.
- Resources in terms of staff, volunteers, management and support for achieving this.
- Related organisational structures and procedures.
- Systems and procedures for monitoring performance against the plan.
- The investment entailed.
- Plans for the longer-term consolidation and development of the gains achieved.

Those responsible for implementation must be prepared to deal with situations that cannot be forecasted, as these arise.

CHAPTER FIVE

Miniature and total strategies

This series of mainly anonymous case studies, and the discussion around them, opens where the author's fundraising began: with church campaigns. This is because these miniature strategies give an overview of strategy in its principles, planning and implementation. These complete but small-scale operations shall be juxtaposed with major national organisations' total strategies aimed at the whole nation, to show that size and complexity do not change the principles, although there are huge differences in the design and execution of strategies between the two scales of organisation.

Miniature strategies: parish appeals

The study preceding a parish appeal or campaign started, as might have been expected, with a review of the capital and recurring needs, which were to be kept distinct. The Finance and General Purposes Committee or an ad hoc committee of the Parochial Church Council, the Kirk Session (in Scotland) or whatever else the responsible body was called would conduct this study, working with a consultant or diocesan adviser. This was part of the procedure introduced by the pioneering Wells: Lew the father and Frank the son.

It sounds easy, and was relatively so in its planning stage, but these campaigns were tense and frantic in implementation. Wells introduced one of their staff as Campaign Director to run them. The preliminary study had to consider the capital, financing, revenue and cash requirements in a universe for fundraising which was often but not always closed: the communion roll, the parish register, the membership, perhaps stretching the closed category to occasional users, who would go to church for baptisms, weddings and funerals. A name on a list or roll was not always a reliable indication of church commitment. And there would be a larger body of prospects where, for example, the building had a civic, community, heritage value beyond its religious functions.

Very often, the strategy had to work within the confines of the parish list or lists. Therefore, in addition to consideration of the needs, there had to be an assessment of the parish's or congregation's capacities for giving and of their likely attitudes to the funding objectives and targets proposed. The case on which this next section will concentrate was in one of the wealthiest Presbyterian parishes in outer Glasgow; but others shall be cited.

If the fundraising study overlooked stresses or conflicts, these would be made acute by the pressures of an intense fundraising campaign. A bad instance of this occurred where the study failed to notice the critical division within a congregation. The ugly, main parish church, which stood beside one of the loveliest buildings in Europe, should have been demolished, but needed substantial capital; as did a proposed, separate parish centre for a prospering suburb. The people in that suburb did not want to support the older, main church, and a rich segment of prospects was lost as a result. In another place, the strategy had been to keep revenue distinct from capital exercises by establishing a separate Building Fund, 'to ensure that bigger givers were able to exercise some control over the manner in which their gifts were used'. The study for this exercise criticised the aggregation of all gifts in a combined fund, because this 'was not in the long-term interests of the parish'. After the study, it was too late to prevent this harm. That campaign was contracted to be run and completed in five weeks, during which time the research had to be completed, the brochure produced, leaders recruited, major support secured, the popular canvass completed, and arrangements for consolidation put in place.

Glasgow: a campaign with two aims

These church-based campaigns were classically designed. The outline that follows is based on a prosperous Glasgow suburb. There was a two-fold aim: to raise £182,000 over seven years to cover recurring expenditure over the seven years (1969–75) and to raise a capital sum of £136,000 to build a new hall for the exclusive benefit of the parish, with no external users. There were about 1,400 households in the congregation, of very different means. Segmentation was defined as laid out over the page.

A capital fund programme for non-recurring needs: £136,000 over seven years

Directed to:	approximately 150 to 200 selected potential donors
Aims:	to break the back of the capital needs
Types and duration of gift:	gifts, bonds of annuity (covenants), interest-free loans, legacies, etc, over a seven- to ten-year period
Timing:	to run for at least three to four months starting on 24 March 1969

A recurring needs (stewardship) programme to raise £182,000 over seven years

Directed to:	the whole congregation, excepting capital fund donors (who would be given an option to contribute to this too)
Aims:	to obtain three-year pledges towards recurring needs, the wider work of the church and to provide a substantial sum towards building costs
Types and duration of gifts:	three-year pledges and seven-year bonds of annuity (covenants)
Timing:	eight to ten weeks starting on the completion of the capital fund programme

The research to identify and evaluate the people to be covered through a personal canvass had a simplicity it would be difficult to match. By the time the research was undertaken, solid agreement should have been reached on the objectives for the campaign. The campaign would aim to cover all members of the congregation, most of whom shared its objectives. In many churches there were rolls or lists of members, although these were sometimes inaccurate and incomplete. Before any process started, there were clues to help in the segmentation of members according to means: houses, their location, occupation, social and recreational activities. Differences in means had to be recognised without giving the suggestion that there was any difference in the value attached to the people.

A confidential Listings Committee was then appointed, consisting of people who could be trusted and who knew the congregation well. Their task was to decide what weekly sum each household (including their own) might afford to give or covenant. The crudest method used was also the most revealing. On the floor around the room, large sheets of paper were placed, each with a proposed weekly sum written on it. There was a card for each household. Cards were discussed in turn and thrown on to one of the sheets. At the end of this process it could be seen from the stacks accumulated whether or not household targets had been pitched at levels which could deliver the campaign's objects. If not, the objects had to be reduced or the household targets raised (with stacks of cards shifted to higher-value sheets). The cards had physically to match the units projected for the number and sizes of gifts needed and to provide a margin allowing for some failures – fewer for churches than for most other causes. This process had several effects: it demonstrated to leaders on the Listings Committee what the unit targets had to be if the campaign was to succeed, and it showed what they themselves should give. It made them convincing advocates for the targets set.

The strategy for that Glasgow campaign targeted the wealthiest households for capital objects; the balance of the households for revenue needs, the running costs of the Kirk – to which the wealthier households would in fact also contribute. This had to be done in a way that would neither create division in the parish nor demean those of lower means, since the object of these programmes was to build unity not division. On the other hand, if the target was to be achieved, the kind of segmentation proposed was necessary. Everyone had to see that they had contributed their fair share towards the measurable costs of church membership and feel that, through whatever level of contribution, they were part owners of the Kirk's capital development. The messages supporting a campaign of this kind had to be framed sensitively. Here, because the new hall was only of use and interest to Kirk members, they had to bear all the costs, with no outside help (this took place many years before the National Lottery).

For the capital programme, units of support from £12,000 down were proposed and illustrated in the appeal brochure. For both the revenue and capital programmes, households were to be visited by a canvasser who was personally, financially committed to the programme. For the 150 to 200 prospects in the capital fund programme, there was a fundraising committee of sixteen, which was not created without difficulty. The first core group, which included four of Glasgow's main company heads, argued that it would be better to raise £1,000 each from their target households – although the minister had already personally pledged £1,500 from a modest salary. Such a formula is inequitable, given the differences between people's means, and almost always fails. In this case, it would have reduced the sums to be given by the core group themselves. As a result, the members of the core group had to be sacked, although this left the campaign bereft of its apparently strongest possible leadership. The crisis had to be declared. If Kirk members wanted to achieve the campaign's objects, they had to trust the strategy and its projected unit targets and they had to find leaders – otherwise the capital part of their programme would fail, and they would not soon have their hall.

Declaration of the crisis produced its solution. Shortly after the collapse of the leadership group, a man close to the programme but not identified as a major prospect (although he knew what the unit targets were) came to the appeal office. He said that he and his wife had recently inherited a large sum of money and wanted to see the Kirk achieve its development programme. They gave £11,000 to the capital programme, validating its unit targets, setting the marker for what should follow and, in the process, giving their leadership.

For the revenue or stewardship programme, a committee of 150 would visit all remaining households. Visitors were not expected to cover more than five to ten households. Part of the brief to visitors was that they should talk explicitly with the families about the sums they might give and indicate what their own families had given. This was an aspect of the leadership role.

Before households were visited, a parish dinner was held in the Glasgow University Refectory which 1,300 people attended, invited and cajoled by a hostess committee, also totalling about 150 members. The purpose was to affirm community, to explain the objects of the campaign and their urgency, to state the funding requirement and how this was to be met. There would be illustration of the units needed and of the ways these could be given, for example by spreading payments over seven years or pledging over three. Weekly, monthly or quarterly giving was recommended, to spread the burden. To show that these were exercises in reality, and that there was committed leadership, interim results were announced, with the statement of some individual contributions.

That campaign had raised more than £320,000 from about 1,500 households over a few months during 1969. That was not the end, however. The strategy declared crucial roles for follow-up and pledge fulfilment committees to ensure as far as possible that sums promised were given; and of a continuation committee, to carry the leadership engaged through the campaign into future development activity.

The report on that Kirk campaign concluded: 'The Capital Fund and Stewardingship programmes are complementary, being a corporate exercise in two parts but the funds they have raised are different and should be managed as such'; the Kirk 'might consider establishing a Trust', partly to show that capital gifts were '. . . being applied according to the donors' intentions'. In other situations, as will be shown presently, the requirement for a trust was acute.

Key characteristics of fundraising in a religious context

Before completing this section, some general points that are relevant in other situations need to be considered. Giving and stewardship in this context (the handling of one's goods as in trust from God) are expressions of religious life. A church is concerned for its members' and others' spiritual welfare, so that generous and responsible giving has intrinsic value, perhaps with neutrality regarding the objects to be supported. There is a series of distinctions to be made for a congregation's financial responsibilities:

- Paying the costs of membership: a calculation can be made for this covering stipends, fees, material and maintenance costs, costs of premises and other overheads if these are for the congregation's exclusive use.

- Meeting a requirement to share one's goods with less fortunate people and communities but not necessarily through a church's outreach programme.

- Meeting the costs for buildings and plant used exclusively by the congregation, with no wider use or interest.

- Meeting the costs for maintaining a building with historic, landmark, heritage significance, which perhaps also serves a community's non-religious needs (for concerts, theatre or other functions) while also serving its residual religious needs for family occasions and Christmas, Easter and Harvest Festival.

Suffolk: fundraising for a long-term solution

In a Suffolk market town, a congregation had two medieval churches, both needing attention to their fabric. The congregation needed only one of the buildings for its worship and could not properly maintain both. A further complication was that another small Anglican congregation in the same town had its own fine, decaying medieval building which it could not afford (Suffolk has more wonderful, costly churches than it has worshippers to support them).

(Some interim points need to be made here. Even where there is an old tradition, the congregation can choose to worship in a costly, historic building, the village hall or a neighbouring shed. The liturgy will be equally valid in any of these. On the other hand, if the church is a landmark building for its community, perhaps one of a town's or village's architectural glories, the values it represents stretch well beyond the congregation. This implied challenge can be made part of the local case for support, whether to occasional users or to non-users who depend on the attraction of the place where they trade or who love the place where they live.)

Returning to Suffolk and the original congregation's two churches, there was no chance of co-operating with the other parish, although this was explored and negotiation started. The two churches were very different in location and history: the older, mother church was away from the town centre, beside the river; the other church was at the top of the famous market place and was its defining feature. It was used for civic functions. The roads around the church were busy and chunks of its fabric were falling on to them.

Already this differs from the situation in Glasgow. That central church was important to the local authority, traders, hoteliers and citizens, regardless of their religious affiliations. In Glasgow the building had been of limited interest and for restricted use. Suffolk's strategic plan and programme had to take advantage of such differences.

The planning study determined that there were capital costs of £70,000 and revenue costs of about £10,000 over three years (this was in 1968 and 1969). The congregation was estimated at around 400. Up to 100 households were to be canvassed for relatively large sums in the capital appeal; 270 households in the revenue appeal. The methods were essentially the same as those used in Glasgow: every household was to be canvassed personally at its appropriate level.

There was also a critical difference in the target publics for the appeal as it related to the church on the market square. The town needed this church more than the congregation did. In those days, such a market town had its own mayor. The plan therefore suggested that the congregation should be responsible for the mother church, where worship could be concentrated, but that responsibility for the town's main church should be shared with the larger universe of people who lived or did business there. There was already a view that the church should be secularised but used for civic services.

The right vehicle had to be designed for this. A Restoration Trust was formed for the main church, its trustees representing the local authority and businesses as well as the parish and diocese. This aspect of the appeal and the Trust itself were chaired by a powerful local businesswoman, who was a dissenter. The Trust was established in such a way that it would have a changing, relevant membership which would continue the community's concern for one of its most conspicuous architectural glories. Trustees included the mayor, the bishop, the rector as well as other main local interests. The congregation would preserve its other, precious mother church.

Families invited to support the revenue programme delivered their target and contributed to the capital fund as they could. This was a *community* enterprise. The capital appeal started in March 1969 and had raised about £71,000 by July of that year, from parish, town, diocesan and civic sources, with additional support coming from national trust and heritage bodies.

More significant for the long term, perhaps, was the fact that seven years later, as covenants were expiring, the trustees were still in place. There was no longer a mayor. The congregation was smaller. The main church on the market square had been secularised. There was another major appeal for an historic building in the town. Despite this, the Trust was there to take the new initiatives. The mother church was also safe.

Dublin: fundraising in a poor parish

There are many variations around the main themes for these parish programmes. A campaign running from late November 1966 to 20 February 1967 had to cover a congregation of almost 4,000 in one of Dublin's poorest parishes. The strategic report concentrated on the 'relatively small number of permanent residents and the relative poverty of this city-centre area', with many flats, boarding houses and bed-sits whose occupancy was constantly changing and where students formed a high proportion of the population. There were not more than twenty households with the means to give more than £100 yearly.

The solution was to secure large numbers of small weekly sums, to deliver a target of £70,000 over the two years. A committee of over 100 men, whose support had been pledged, agreed to visit every parish household (3,876 visits were made). There was a women's committee of about 150 to organise two dinners at which the case for support would be made before large-scale visiting began. A total of 2,650 people came to the dinners, which were held late in January.

To ensure that people came and left on time, specially chartered trains brought the guests to and from Bray, a seaside town just outside Dublin, where the dinners were held in the Arcadia Ballroom. By the time visiting was completed the following month, £62,000 had been raised through weekly giving, which ranged from £4 to less than 2/6 (12½p). Administrative records were installed. The report commented: 'the period of intense canvassing that has just ended is only the beginning of the long-term programme', which was the responsibility of the Continuation Committee.

KEY PRINCIPLES IN SUMMARY

These miniature appeals express the basic principles for any fundraising strategy:

- Establish the needs.
- Identify and evaluate the universes of potential support.
- Articulate the reasons why different parts of the universe should give support at appropriate levels.
- Find the methods to realise prospects' potential and deliver the targets.
- Deploy the resources demanded by these methods.
- Install records and procedures to secure the future.

Total strategies: reaching the nation

The next kind of strategy to be considered aims at the whole conscious nation and assumes a great cause with universal appeal – children, heart disease, cancer, world poverty and environment – as distinct from causes that are problematic, such as mental disability, AIDS, young offenders or causes that may be of interest only to larger or smaller parts of the total population, such as higher education, heritage objects, opera, birds or regional causes. A further assumption is that the organisation for which the strategy is being designed has the capability to deliver the services demanded by the great cause, through enhancement or re-direction, and that it has at least the minimal skills on which a massive funding programme may be built. The material that follows is based on real cases.

Design of the strategic plan can start from very different points. There may be a need that can be determined with fair accuracy: a defined project such as Great Ormond Street Hospital, Tate Modern, the Royal Opera House or the new University for Lincolnshire would be examples. Or there may simply be an opportunity to make revolutionary advances against some great need, for which it is initially impossible to determine the sum needed so that the targets, when first set, are somewhat arbitrary. This section will concern itself with the latter situation. The first section of this chapter, for personal and historical reasons, dealt with situations thirty years ago: church programmes are no longer run so rigorously, but the strategies used then were seminal. This next section deals with current affairs.

The fundraising situation seems arbitrary when it starts with raw opportunity; but there are at once factors that will contribute to the direction of strategic planning. If the cause has weight and the organisation credibility, given a situation in which all fundraising is brutally competitive, there are two early points to be made about targets for an intended major funding programme as its planning begins:

- If the needs demand a large-scale programme, and the organisation, within limits, can deliver services on any scale demanded, then the overall target must mark this as *the* appeal or one of the few key appeals for the period into which it is launched.

- The overall target must be large enough to permit prospects and appeal segments to contribute at or near their potential. If a single source is needed for, say, £10 million, this must be seen as one unit among many contributing to a much greater achievement – unless the strategy says that one unit of £10 million has to deliver the whole programme. Similarly, the overall target must allow Manchester or Bristol to deliver £5 million, if this is their appropriate target, and not set a £250,000 target which is below these places' potential or the programme's needs. The regional or sector gift table should reflect the national table, not replace it.

Those generalisations, however accurate, must not get in the way of a more potent issue. No funding programme should be based on a crude demand for support. It may not be artificial. The cause must be weighty. The programme should be capable of delivering very significant responses to the needs, which would otherwise be unattainable. The great appeal should be inspired by the great idea.

If, given no determined object (such as a building or specific programme), the strategic plans start with opportunity and a great cause, they must quickly base themselves on solid needs and principles. Some programmes have started with fingers held in the air, testing the wind and considering directions. At that moment we might say: 'A target of £Xm would be appropriate and would claim a dominant national position for the appeal.' There might be back-of-envelope-figures and conjectures around this, and the development of bold hypotheses. Then serious strategic planning began.

The processes that follow are complex, vary from organisation to organisation and depend on context and situations. The next chapter will consider situations for organisations of other kinds which cannot assume nationwide awareness and assent. The process on which this chapter concentrates is the design of a strategic plan, the assumption being that there will be a nine-figure target but that the studies through which various high-level strategies are designed can have different aims. For example:

- To convince the trustees that the massive initiative proposed is necessary and feasible.

- Or, if it has been decided to take the initiative, to examine the programmes to be mounted and to design the fundraising strategies to support them.

Despite these differences, there are broad similarities between the investigative and planning activities. It is important to bear in mind that the planning process cannot remove doubt or eliminate risk. That can only be done by running and achieving the strategy, or failing to do so. Planning includes judgements on risk and on its control and management. Every strategy's implementation is subject to chance, circumstance, bad tactical judgement and good fortune. The best strategic plan leaves the organisation in the real, fickle, changeable world.

The case: beginnings

A difficulty often arises when precise service programmes have not been determined as planning begins. Evidently, a massive programme of the kind considered here must be based on service. It cannot be just about money. One exercise to be undertaken early during the planning study, among a series of parallel exercises, is to engage people within the organisation who are responsible for services. They may not previously have been asked to think on this scale and may be sceptical about the possibility of delivering the proposed funding targets. They are unlikely to understand fundraising and may even resent dependence on voluntary funding and distrust its richer sources. A frequent, early response, already mentioned, is: 'Tell us what you can raise money for, and we'll package something for you.' A new fundraiser introduced for such an appeal in a great organisation recently commented: 'When I arrived as a fundraiser, I expected the pressure of the job to be the demands made by colleagues in programmes to secure large amounts of funding for their programmes. In fact, the pressure of the job is the daily struggle to persuade my colleagues to have the confidence in their work to seek the endorsement and support of the outside world.'

Do not yet despair. It is vital that the programmes should be agreed, costed and explained. In the cases on which this chapter is drawing, funding on the scale proposed was essential if the opportunity to deliver huge benefits was to be grasped, and there was real, not artificial, demand for achievement. The service staff – social workers, environmentalists, academics – had therefore to be brought along so that they saw, and were motivated by, the mission and believed sufficiently in the fundraising to be inspired not just to respond but to co-operate. This kind of exercise can take time, patience and understanding from the staff and consultants carrying out a planning study, if they are to succeed and inter-departmental relations to improve. Even then, development of service programmes may not proceed at the pace needed by the critical timetable for the planning exercise. This means that, in addition to briefings, discussions, meetings and cajolings, there must also be senior management support for the process, with backing from trustees, as well as peer pressure for progress from the finance committee, steering group or management board. Situations vary between organisations. This may be an aspect of good fortune: two recent, simultaneous assignments involved, on the one hand, a chairman of trustees who was the main, nervous brake on progress where the rest of the trustees wanted to move on and, on the other hand, a chairman who turned out to be the most visionary person involved in planning basic reform of the way the organisation should operate. Of the two, the latter had significantly higher corporate and social standing. Fortunate situations may also be planned: a team may be put in place within the organisation to plot, argue and worry through the internal and external processes needed to deliver a timely outcome.

Even when the service programmes have been determined, there may be the further issue of rendering these programmes into a case for support that can be used externally, especially where understanding depends on considerable background knowledge or where internal communications make extensive use of jargon, institutional shorthands or codes. No outsider should be expected to know what these might mean or to understand 'major support', 'prospects' or that asininity 'the ask'. The internal statement may need to be translated into a language and style that intelligent outsiders would find interesting.

What is needed at this stage is an accurate and motivating declaration of the national or worldwide cause and a description of how the organisation proposes to respond to the needs, in ways that will have impact on them. This document could be produced by development staff, with agreement from their service colleagues. The statement of case that is generated in this way will be well-founded but incomplete, with only provisional estimates of costs, and open to change as informed outsiders are drawn into the process, partly through its vision and logic.

Initial verification of appeal objects and of potential

Let us assume a situation where the board, management and senior staff are sceptical about the possibility of raising a nine-figure sum and do not absolutely believe that their organisation is either able to achieve this or to deliver the services that would then have to be delivered. Despite this, having been briefed, they have had confidence enough to authorise the planning study. This raises a series of questions which had to be answered to give confidence to the strategy. For example:

- Has any such target previously been delivered in the UK? The answer is factual. Many organisations have over time raised sums running into nine figures; a few have raised sums between £100 million and £300 million through concentrated programmes, most prominently Oxford and Cambridge universities. The Royal Opera House engaged on a similar programme. These are, however, eminent academic and arts institutions; welfare, third world and environmental agencies have until now accumulated their substantial support more gradually. Nevertheless, experience shows that welfare organisations have taken initiatives over the past decade to match the higher levels of achievement from other sectors, with a demonstrated capacity to raise their performance to new dimensions. Good fundraising changes the realities. Consequently, where there is a great cause, the initial presupposition must be that previous highest levels of achievement can at least be matched. It is a sound instinct that in a potent situation previous levels of achievement can be significantly exceeded; that this may in itself provide strong reasons for backers' participation.

- Can units of support at the levels needed realistically be projected? A target of £100 million, for example, will demand some units of support between £10 million and £20 million. There are many examples of such generosity and attainment. Units between £1 million and £5 million are commoner. Such figures have been increasing. So, if the cause and programmes carry national or international weight, they must in principle be capable of attracting such support. Note also that a total strategy of the kind considered here assumes some units will be raised from large numbers of relatively smaller contributions, for example, through employee giving, promotions, direct marketing, events and more popular techniques.

■ Can we reach the people and institutions who could support us at this level? This will evidently partly depend on the strength and perceived importance of the case and the responsive programmes proposed; but the kinds of established organisations under discussion here have initial advantages. Their past and current patrons, presidents, friends, and selected supporters should provide routes through which they can persuade some main backers to increase support and lead them to new high potential prospects, bringing existing networks and hopefully new advocates into play.

Even when those broad questions can be answered satisfactorily, a crucial issue remains: are there the sources that can support the enterprise at the levels projected? Answers to this question are more complicated. Let us assume a cause and case capable of motivating responses from the whole universe of possible support, with all its segments in principle available for this appeal (certain causes, which do not apply here, would have more restrictive criteria for selection). There will be limits to activity where resources cannot be stretched to exploit a particular segment or where cost benefits will be inadequate.

Planning the research

This is where a battery of research methods will be employed. The research starts with a review of past performance, often more difficult than it sounds. At the start of this part of the exercise, it is found that the data stored do not permit adequate regressive analysis, so that cumulative levels of support from single sources cannot be measured without recourse to less easily retrieved archival material. It is also found that records within the organisation are fragmented between corporate, trust, high-level donors, trading and the mass of supporters on direct marketing lists. It later emerges that records of previous major appeals are incomplete. The history of these achievements have to be unsatisfactorily filled out from the memories of a diminishing number of people who were around some years ago. The fundraising regions are mostly reluctant to share their records, and some effectively prevent any transfer of information. Yet it is necessary to have as complete a history as possible of past fundraising performance, including many sources that have given well above £100,000 and a few that have given more than £1 million. It is assumed that the appeal will enhance all segments of fundraising, and that the past sets no limit on the future. Eventually, the research reveals maps of the connections between people who can become networkers for the appeal. It also includes the records of ordinary, regular supporters and, from market research and personal contacts, descriptions of them. This internal review is carried out by staff, perhaps with some guidance from a consultant and later with input from external research agencies.

The external research has huge scope, but one of its first aims is to establish that there are sufficient prospects in principle capable of supporting a major appeal at the levels projected. There are now several published listings of the rich, all incomplete and to some extent inaccurate, but they provide a base on which to build. Lists can be bought for many other categories of supporters, but most lists are imperfect, and the information they contain is soon out of date. Supplements to the various forms of published knowledge can be obtained through contacts generated by the appeal's progress, through luck or vigilance, and also through contrivance and subterfuge.

So far, the research processes as described are normal; it is the demands of a £100 million appeal that make them exceptional. The process has identified the high-level prospects capable of giving over £1 million. Answering the questions 'Who can give £1 million?' and 'Who has given over £1 million?' provides a useful clue to prospects' future action, but is not a determinant of it. Part of the strategy is to change the behaviour of all types of prospects. At the top levels this means finding new donors of tens and hundreds of thousands as well as millions of pounds. Other organisations' appeals have achieved this. At lower levels the appeal is to lift donors from hundreds to thousands of pounds or from tens to hundreds.

There is an important distinction to be made again here. Information may be gathered:

- to provide a basis for judgement and decision, or
- to target and direct action.

The rest of this section will focus primarily on the first of these.

The research

At this stage of the research, there could be a limited exercise in profiling, with outline details on selected prospects and detailed profiling on an even more carefully selected, smaller number of these. This is partly a demonstration exercise to show how the networks of contacts available to people already closely associated with the organisation give it access to those who can deliver the higher levels of funding needed. The intention is to illustrate what can already be achieved, not to complete the mapping of networks, which will be done later if the programme proceeds.

Several strands of research are run simultaneously with those profiling exercises:

- The research will identify: the trusts or foundations that are conduits for personal or family giving; those where it is useful to reach one or more trustees; and those that must be approached formally through their directors, secretaries, administrators, correspondents. An informed view will be taken on a likely result from these sources, given the networks for contacts available, the strength of the propositions and the pressure of public opinion that are intended.

- An assessment is made of the ways companies can be involved in what is planned as an overwhelmingly popular campaign, whether or not the company's decisive decision-maker is to be personally involved. Companies too need to be offered methodologies and themes for delivering significant corporate support. Usually, it is only through the active personal involvement of corporate leaders that optimal results will be secured from this sector. There are exceptions, though. For example, corporate and commercial interests would be the crucial factor if a pharmaceutical company wanted to base laboratories on a famous campus, or an IT company wanted to use the same facilities to gain access to advanced knowledge and technology. Most of the seven-figure sums delivered by companies, however, have required a considerable degree of personal leadership, as well as pragmatism, for there to be success in achieving a decision to give support at the level needed. Once leadership has been engaged, there must be flexibility on the ways support can be given: grants, sponsorships, joint promotions, employee giving are options that may be combined to deliver significant support for a single cause. It is therefore important to assess an organisation's ability to reach and involve main companies in its enterprise and also to consider the forms of support it can offer and service. The latter point is significant: one major appeal made the judgement that the charity's nationwide network of support groups could service in-store promotions worth over £1 million. This turned out to be quite humiliatingly wrong, and the company asked if the appeal needed help from a charity with more co-operative local supporters. The appraisal has to be pitilessly realistic.

- Much potential for giving is regionally or locally based and can often be released only if a local or regional benefit will ensue. Many regional people and organisations want to be part of a national enterprise, with some justice: if they were not, there would be no transfer of resources from rich to poor places, and Eaton Square would be overwhelmed with unwanted facilities. A separate issue is the patchy reluctance of some regions to divulge their own useful information for use within the total strategy. Nevertheless, the research has to consider what the regions could deliver and where larger or smaller investment is to be made. The potentialities and demands from Manchester or Leeds or Bristol or the West Midlands, for example, are different from those from the south-east and London or from Wiltshire, Hereford, Shropshire, Cumbria and the south-west. Information is needed on individual, corporate and trust sources for the regions and on the ways leadership operates in each place – through social, corporate, sporting or religious networks. Many regions have directories of their corporate and individual rich; journalists, estate agents and others have useful, if selective, information; the organisation's people know much, if they will share their knowledge. At the end of this process, recommendations have to be made on whether and how such appeals will be run – regionally or locally controlled, nationwide or selectively, in a few places only? The study will have to recommend what resources are needed to deliver the regional programmes, through re-training and re-equipping staff, introduction of new staff or both; and what returns on investment may be reckoned for this aspect of an appeal.

■ The direct marketing programme is to be boosted in the numbers to be involved and the levels and regularity of contributions. There may be new propositions concerning the ways funds are solicited and the regularity of payments, perhaps drawing on the church models of family, weekly or monthly giving. Some research will profile current donors in terms of the usual broad demographic and lifestyle criteria; qualitative research will search out new categories of prospects, given the major new programme to be launched; there will be a search for new lists which may be productive. Given that there are new publics and propositions to be explored, one argument is for there to be quite elaborate testing before new, large-scale direct marketing programmes are launched; but the counter-argument is that there can be no reliable testing outside the context of the vast publicity and promotional campaign. This can only be mounted when it has been decided to undertake the total programme, and then only at the right time within that programme. (This does not mean, however, that some of the qualitative research exercises that are also being undertaken cannot be used.)

Qualitative research

Other research can only be started when the first version of the case has been prepared with the arguments for the appeal. This research has two main parts:

■ Individual interviews.

■ Focus groups.

Uses of qualitative research

Such qualitative investigation can be used with a number of selected people and with a variety of purposes, principally to establish the level of understanding of the arguments and propositions and, more significantly, the responses and attitudes they evoke. These exercises provide important information, can play a useful role in the involvement of fundraising leaders and opinion-makers and can be influential in determining a decision from the board and senior management. They are also, however, perilous because, being based on unrepresentative samples too small to give a statistically probable result, they can express minority, selective views. Their results have to be used carefully.

At its broadest level, the qualitative research probes the responses of general supporters, of different types and in different parts of the country, to some of the main messages and propositions intended for the more popular segments of the appeal. Procedures for this are familiar and well-proven and are more likely to guide than mislead experienced marketing and fundraising practitioners. The qualitative exercise includes focus groups, run by research specialists, with regional people and some established main donors. It is usually best to deal separately with different categories of supporters.

It is when qualitative research is applied to the major support segments and to people who may influence public opinion that its use is most delicate. This exercise is in research not fundraising, but it does change opinion and engage interest. What is being sought is a response to the message, a view, desirably some clues or indications of support – but not a commitment. The exercise must not induce hostile rejection. Such qualitative investigation will involve visits by staff (with or without a consultant) to key individuals, using agreed drafts of the case statement and plan, to try to establish what they think about these and whether they might participate if asked to do so (major national figures will be visited by the organisation's chair or director, after careful briefing). Some of these people will be possible main donors or leaders; others might in due course be asked to endorse the programme. The research itself can be part of a process for their involvement.

Initial verification of capabilities and of costs

The organisation has by now accumulated a mass of information, sufficient to provide a basis for judgement. The process has been extensive but not exhaustive. Complete lists, profiles, network maps will be prepared only if the decision is made to proceed, and even then only close to the time for their use.

Yet there are further questions to be answered. Are the structures for implementation of this strategy suitable for the enterprise? The outline analysis given below is an ordinary example, illustrating the issues:

FIGURE 3 OUTLINE ANALYSIS OF FUNCTIONS

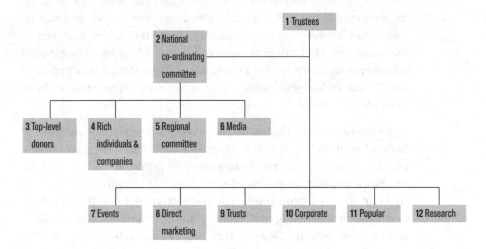

1 The trustees have ultimate, inalienable responsibility for policies and action.

2 There is a national co-ordinating committee on which the trustees and main appeal committees are represented. This might meet three or four times during the intense appeal.

3 Top-level donors represent the highest levels of wealth and may only meet once, informally.

4 Rich individuals with their trusts or foundations and companies have their own co-ordinating group, which would meet regularly during the intense campaign; sectional sub-groups operate within its scope and are represented on it.

5 The many regional sub-committees are represented, co-ordinated and supported through the main regional committee.

6   The media group will be active during the intense campaign and influential with the media, in addition to the organisation's routine advertising and PR.

7   An events resource may be needed to service volunteer groups and to take its own initiatives, co-operatively with national appeal activities.

8   The organisation's direct marketing must be co-ordinated with the rest of the activities. The existing high-value donor base is also to be extended, with levels of contributions raised.

9   There is a specialist function responsible for trusts or foundations which falls outside the scope of the national co-ordinating committee and is also there for handling any detailed action required by that committee.

10   There are opportunities for negotiation with companies that fall outside the scope of the national co-ordinating committee.

11   Given that this appeal is aimed at the whole population, there will be more popular fundraising: collections, schools, churches, sponsored activity, and trading.

12   Research and records will be continuing functions.

Those functions determine a series of task descriptions. With an active organisation, there are people already in post: are they adequate for the new tasks? The people involved in functions 9 and 10 may be very good at their present jobs, but can they cope with functions 3 and 4? Existing regional staff are effective in current fundraising but lack skills for major support programmes. Some new staff will have to be brought in for the appeal, on salary or contract; some existing staff will need training; others will have to be transferred. These are management decisions which call on the resources of the personnel department and, on some matters, for the use of outside advice. The ways such moves are handled are an aspect of the management of change.

Investment

A second, related matter is the budget. Given decisions on the actions to be taken, the resources these demand and the sequence of activity defined by the timetable, it is now possible to project the scale and incidence for costs of all kinds, with the anticipated inflow of funds as well as pledges from the appeal. But the judgements that have to be made on those projections are a cause of further problems. For a target above £100 million, investment may reach £10 million. A sum above £3 million may have to be spent before returns are seen on initial investment. These sums are beyond the experience of most, but not all, of the trustees. It may not be understood, for example, that a long preparatory period is essential before major support begins to flow or that there may be no instant solicitations for funds. Equally, it may not be understood that acquisition of donors through direct marketing takes time. A cold list will seldom warm up rapidly. These matters will have to be explained to trustees and reassurances given based on fact and experience. Such moments for reappraisal are allowed for in the timetable, which should include a monitoring process and, at points before large-scale fundraising is launched, 'gates' for decisions to be made to continue, to stop or to redirect all or parts of the programme. Such investment has to be shown to be necessary if the organisation is to achieve its service goals, and precedents must be presented which show that the investment also carries a reasonable probability of being productive. (Good decisions and sound judgement of this kind cannot be based on certainties.)

There is a separate issue for a total fundraising strategy of this kind. The general principle is that every method used must deliver a cost benefit, but in this instance the organisation is undertaking a campaign which needs to draw broad public assent and co-operation. A gift to this great cause shows that the donor wants to associate with it, with a degree of understanding, however minimal. Therefore, as a means of drawing the broadest possible assent to vision and mission, there may be justification for some fundraising exercises which simply cover their costs.

Finally, the strategic plan already considers how supporters of all kinds will be acknowledged, how more significant supporters will be recognised and how the involvement of at least a few will be sustained and consolidated after the appeal has been completed.

Conclusion: the decision

For the time being we will continue to concentrate on situations where the planning study must provide grounds for deciding whether or not to proceed, and in what direction (towards the end of the chapter we will return to the situation where a decision has already been taken to proceed so that the requirement is for a strategy for prompt action).

The planning study having been completed, the toil of persuasion begins. The report and its supporting papers are of critical importance here. The main text must be long enough to present the findings and argument convincingly, but short enough to be read, not skimmed. This means that the full detail supporting each point will not be given in the text (this detail is given in a series of addenda or appendices to which reference can be made by anyone wanting the fuller facts). Additionally, the research findings must be listed and tabulated in a separate document because of their bulk. There are different contributors to the addenda, appendices, supplements as well as to the main report text. Management, policy, service delivery, personnel as well as fundraising divisions have all contributed. The report must, however, have some unifying authorship if it is to be coherent. These papers have objective roles, guiding and underpinning judgements. They also surely have a polemic role since there is an unstated presupposition that the organisation's services, and consequently its funding, must together make a great leap forward. The facts may not be distorted, but the argument tends towards a desired conclusion, although this intention may remain concealed and will be denied quite honestly by most of the report's contributors. Alternatively, the argument may be to abort the enterprise.

There has to be a process which gives space and time but also sets deadlines for decision making. If the cause is urgent so is the process. The decision is of such importance, and its implications so costly, demand for time falls outside the trustees' and management's routine schedules. Further, because decision making is a human process, it creates factions. The proposed programmes are daunting and require inside, informed allies. There are some trustees and others close to the organisation who are well disposed towards the initiative and want to be part of it. There is also an opposing faction. So it is sensible and constructive to let the programme's allies in, so that they can challenge and ask questions about it, equipping themselves as its internal advocates. At the same time, there must be confidence that management, service and fundraising have the conviction and will to carry through the programmes for which they will be responsible. All this implies the presence of people within the organisation who combine vision, idealism and opportunism sufficient to launch, for example, a crusade involving the whole population which, fuelled by fundraising, will outlaw one of our society's great evils or radically change the international approach to sustainable growth.

Given the weight of responsibility these trustees will have to bear (which we hope they understand) they must be provided with a context in which they can reach judgement responsibly: they must be presented with clear information and arguments, given the opportunity to question and challenge them, and allowed the time to consider their conclusions, with a deadline for these. They must be given a heavy body of study documents, although most will read only the main report and the additional material that interests them. There is an issue about security here: the material they have been given is confidential, the information has been expensively gained, and some of the trustees are also involved with other, more or less competitive organisations. There are no absolute safeguards, but documents can be numbered and returned and confidentiality urged.

Implementation

Once it has been decided to go ahead, there is a complexity of activity to be initiated. This starts with selected, progressive communication of the intention to proceed so that people needing privileged notice will get this early but nobody feels they were neglected or that they heard late and by accident. In this context, there is a point to be made about the qualitative interviews with key possible supporters, leaders and advocates. These were earlier described as static, isolated in time; but, if they are, their impact dwindles and can even end by turning negative. In a programme where the decision making has become protracted, it is quite likely that the prospects who were first interviewed (and who responded positively) will have lost interest and recall by the time the organisation returns to them. The main purpose of that qualitative interview may have been objective, but it was also part of a dynamic process, leading from theoretical study to action. Many of the people who were interviewed as part of the study need privileged information on the decisions to proceed, and some of them need prompt invitation to enter active roles. They are all to be part of a great, planned conspiracy for good.

The outcomes are interestingly different, largely because of the very different degrees of commitment generated within these organisations.

Variable strategies

This chapter considers a range of strategies for appeals in organisations of different sizes and types in order to show how principles are shared while their applications must be sensitive and flexible. Here again a few miniature programmes will be cited as well as programmes on a large scale.

The great institution

In most countries, there are a few institutions and places which carry the highest international as well as national esteem: Venice, Athens, Petra; the Smithsonian, the Uffizi, the Louvre; Canterbury, Santa Sophia, the Dome of the Rock; Harvard and Yale, Oxford and Cambridge. Important in themselves, these may also offer glory through association. There are few places where people can create an outstandingly visible, lasting memorial, or which embody enduring excellence. Where an appeal relates to such a place and institution, extraordinary factors can be invoked.

In this respect, Oxford and Cambridge have advantages which other universities lack, over and above their rich and extensive alumni lists. In the recent past, but before the appeals described here were launched, benefactors who had little to do with universities and nothing to do with Oxbridge have funded colleges, quadrangles and chairs, quite apart from the self interest which motivates some corporate support for a department or specific research facility.

The strategic plan developed for Cambridge in 1989 postulated two objectives:

- to raise £250 million over ten years, a target unprecedented at the time;
- to create habits, mechanisms and procedures to secure regular long-term income for the University.

The total target was originally set as a horizon, with £120 million in specific medium-term goals.

The University's Council of Senate had already agreed that a foundation be established to give authority to the campaign, to provide status and involvement for some powerful individuals from outside the University and to create a secure but separate receptacle for funds. This was an important element in the strategy, for the immediate programmes and for the University's independent long-term funding. The foundation was to devolve fundraising responsibilities to a main committee for major support and to another for graduates' big gifts. Separate initiatives were to be taken for covering overseas sources and the balance of alumni.

The context for this appeal was recognised to be complex. The University already raised about £25 million yearly, mainly in research grants (which were assiduously kept out of its announced appeal totals, although Oxford added them in). There were 40 appeals being run by colleges and other independent points within the University. Cambridge as a corporate body was perceived to be rich and, as the appeal started, questions were asked about its fiscal management. A few colleges were rich; many more were believed to be so. Oxford was known to be mounting an appeal of its own, so here was a demand for half a billion pounds from two already highly privileged institutions. Were rich elitists being invited to fund elitism? They were.

Segmentation of the prospects was designed to reflect the special make-up of Cambridge's body of alumni. There were three upper tiers, targeted as follows in terms of unit targets and numbers of prospects:

- £50 million to £1 million from 26 sources with 80–100 prospects.
- £999,999 to £50,000 from 215 sources with 650 prospects.
- Many prosperous sources targeted for between £5,000 and £50,000, and for legacies.

Long-term procedures were also eventually to be introduced to secure support from a high proportion of Cambridge graduates.

The plan proposed creation of an established, computerised research function within the development office: 'There will be a continuing requirement for prospect research.' Research was vital from the start. Although there was a complete survey and listing of rich and prosperous Cambridge graduates, it was clear that the processes used could not catch them all. The first occasion, a reception hosted by Sir Geoffrey (now Lord) Howe, was followed up personally, to test responses and to see who might join the appeal team. An early focus for the appeal's activity was to be a reception at Buckingham Palace, hosted by the Duke of Edinburgh, the Chancellor of the University, for which a list was being researched to identify prospects with exceptional means. These prospects were to be approached personally by people at the highest level within the University. Research has remained an expert function within the Cambridge development office.

This appeal had a highly intelligent and diplomatically skilled development director. But its driving force was the foundation, chaired by Sir Alastair Pilkington with Sir Adrian Cadbury as deputy. Sir Alastair insisted that neither he nor the foundation was to be directly responsible for the fundraising. Nevertheless, he immediately led an essential process: the clarification and statement of the reasons why Cambridge had to mount this appeal. There were many people who questioned the need for this, more usually those who felt threatened than those whose support was to be engaged. The plan proposed: 'The first task has to be a vigorous articulation of the arguments supporting the Cambridge appeal' and 'There must be no bland recital of aspirations. Statements must be based on credible plans, and they must be ordered according to their priority ("Now critical"/ "Urgent"/"Highly desirable")'. Without Sir Alastair's persistence and the development director's negotiating skills, the task would have been overwhelming, demanding as it did that each faculty should argue its own case for support. It was understood that there could not be perfect precision and clarity, but a £250 million target, never yet undertaken in the UK, had to be made credible and intelligible. In the end, supported by a strong argument for the overall appeal, the horizon of need was set at £250 million, with explicit programmes totalling about £120 million having priority.

It was on this basis that the presentation was prepared for the Chancellor's reception. The earliest shortlists of leadership prospects had already included four of the sources that were eventually to give between £1 million and £5 million. Research for the Chancellor's function added many more, including a new source which would provide £8 million. There was a moment before the higher sums were achieved when an emergency session of the key players was assembled over dinner. Some commitments between £1 million and £1.5 million had been made, several of those around the table contributing at this level. Using the projection of the scales of support and numbers of units needed, it had to be shown that, although these were extraordinary results, they did not measure up to a £250 million achievement. As the strategy approached its first public launches, it became urgent that those early markers be provided. They were.

Nevertheless, the Cambridge strategy did not operate perfectly to plan. At the point when the appeal was beginning to gather pace, and despite the fact that it was achieving unprecedentedly high results, it still had no fundraising chairman. Sir Alastair continued, effectively but reluctantly, to drive the appeal from his position as foundation chairman. In addition, segmentation of the alumni was not carried through as proposed.

A great institution of international standing cannot take it for granted that its position will earn support. One of the great Royal Colleges had a standing appeal committee that would have been envied by most institutions, but it was burdened by a research institute which it wanted to shed. Adjoining its fine main building was a building of less distinction, which had high real estate value but was being used as a hostel at the time. Its sale would have met the College's quite serious needs.

The College was seen by many non-members as a trade union for an already privileged profession, whose members were almost universally financially committed elsewhere. For some time the appeal committee had done nothing, its sessions making no difference to affairs, and its members saying that, while they attended out of courtesy, the College had low priority for their personal and corporate philanthropy. The proposal was that this committee be stood down at a luncheon which thanked them and acknowledged their good will. Then new opportunities for fundraising might be considered; or other funding options addressed.

There are obviously big differences between the fundraising situations for Oxford and Cambridge and those of most other universities. Some, such as Manchester, Durham, Leeds, Edinburgh, Trinity Dublin, St Andrews and London, have strong lists of alumni but which still do not match those for Oxbridge. Many provide teaching and research of the highest quality, and some attract strong regional loyalties. Many, more especially among the newly-formed universities, have as yet few rich or famous alumni and have to work very hard to establish networks of contacts through which they can reach the people they need to persuade for support, or those who might influence them.

FULL STOP: the total appeal

The objective of NSPCC's FULL STOP campaign has been to eliminate child abuse in the UK within a generation. This has entailed a redeployment and restructuring of NSPCC's services for children at risk and their families. The appeal's objective has been to raise the additional funds required for NSPCC to achieve its service objectives.

Thinking about this started by 1994. In 1995 it was realised that a huge increase in voluntary funding would be needed to deliver the campaign's and appeal's objectives. Detailed preliminary planning for the appeal, paralleling planning for services, started in October 1995 and culminated in March 1996. It was then anticipated that the appeal would have to raise at least £100m.

A strategy for services was presented to NSPCC's trustees early in 1997. That part of the planning process showed that, allowing for normal growth in established income, an additional £250m would be needed over the ten years 2000 to 2010. If there was to be an end to child abuse, NSPCC, to extend and reinforce services, would need such a sum. The fundraising strategy, designed to deliver it, and based on an unprecedentedly exacting study, was agreed in the spring of 1997.

The fundraising study involved internal staff and also external experts and agencies, with massive leadership and prospect research exercises. It covered the targets, the case, the prospective sources, the required leadership, organisation and structure, procedures for solicitation, monitoring and consolidation, as well as internal and external communications and cooperation. The timetable assumed £24m in gifts and pledges raised early in 1999, with the bulk of funds raised during 1999/2000.

The target was massive for the UK and had only previously been achieved here by Oxford and Cambridge Universities, institutions of a completely different kind from NSPCC. In the UK as in the USA, the very large unit sums that must be raised to secure such sums within a sensible timespan have gone to the great cultural and arts bodies, not to welfare organisations. The fundraising challenge NSPCC took on, aiming to match the multi-million units of support those other bodies raised, was extraordinary. Some possible leaders were and remain sceptical about the likelihood of its achievement. Other leaders remain committed to achieve it: because, surely, the safeguarding of all our children from abuse is more important than the funding of our great cultural and educational institutions.

The overall and unit targets for the FULL STOP appeal were boldly set at levels achieved by those institutions. The trustees and the appeal leadership, having challenged the fundraising study and the strategy based on it, agreed to the challenge and the risk. NSPCC was encouraged by the fact that, in its 1984 Centenary Appeal, it had set and exceeded even the highest levels of giving for welfare agencies at that time, establishing a model that others followed.

The results to date, for this Total Appeal, should already shift perceptions of what can be achieved. FULL STOP has again changed the accepted realities and possibilities for welfare fundraising. This reflects the quality of NSPCC's Appeals Directorate and staff. For example:

- The direct marketing programme acquired about 50,000 additional donors and by 2000/2001 had raised at least a new £25m.
- 30 units above £1m have delivered about £50m.
- 84 units between £100,000 and £1m have delivered over £20m from 'prosperous' sources.
- Regional appeals have raised £25m to date.

Those were the results, in cash and pledges, of the appeal's first phase. The original model was for an intensive appeal which would run for one year, because it was believed the leadership would only commit for that period. However, because, within the original strategy, internal resources and external structures were in place, and FULL STOP's intention and direction are clear, the second phase has been launched with refreshed leadership. This refreshed leadership has taken a longer time horizon but retains the original aspiration. Over £100m has been raised, which is already delivering new services for the protection of children. And new markers have been set for welfare fundraising in the UK.

Regional and local appeals

Regional or even local appeals need not be on a small scale but it may be useful to reduce the size of the cause considered in order to clarify fundamentals again. The case that starts this section is small and starkly clear: in a medium-sized town a few people came together for an unpopular cause, to provide a place where single, pregnant women could opt to go if they did not want to be under pressure to have an abortion. A building had been offered by the council, and fees would cover running costs. That left £30,000 to be raised to equip the house and make it pleasantly habitable.

Poor unmarried mothers are an unpopular cause and may not be welcome neighbours, so the case was tested on a number of possible prospects, who rejected it. The appeal therefore had to succeed through the contributions of a small group with unequal means, all of whom passionately wanted the facility to be provided. They were convinced of the case but had not been confronted with its implications in terms of the funding each must provide. Since only twenty to thirty people were involved, this could be achieved through a short, blunt session at which the sums needed and the ways these could be given (using a tax-benefited umbrella body) were explained. There had to be at least one unit of £5,000, two of £3,000, five of £2,000 and several over £1,000. The total was quickly delivered. The method for achieving it was classical: a strong case and clear targets delivered to a universe of prospects whose motives were clearly understood.

Compared to the figures used elsewhere in this book, the sums involved in this appeal were small, and its benefit was strictly limited geographically. However, the principles remain the same, and, in relation to the giving potential of the people involved, the achievement was just as significant. During the fifteen years I have lived here, my home villagers have raised about £1m for a hall, sports pitch and pavilion, swimming pool and church; all through carefully segmented appeals, in addition to high-yielding, weekly, popular appeals.

The second appeal to be considered was to establish the first residential centre of its kind for Alzheimer's sufferers, to serve communities in an urban, industrial area of the north-east of England. It was estimated that there were 11,000 people with Alzheimer's in the area, which was already served by the organisation's day-care facilities. The appeal objective was to fund a nursing home with a day centre and an administrative unit attached, offering progressive provision on one site, moving from day care to short-term residential to long-term residential care. The service was aimed at carers as well as sufferers, providing respite relief.

The total cost of the project (this was in 1990) was estimated at £1.4 million. The regional Development Corporation offered £500,000 and the county and borough councils were targeted for £200,000 and £60,000 respectively. A fundraising target of £750,000 was therefore proposed. The appeal was planned to run over 15 months from the moment the strategic plan and targets were agreed. In addition to the sources mentioned and the health authority, principal prospects identified were main regional companies and major national and regional trusts.

The method proposed included 'the creation of a small, highly influential group of financially committed leaders who would accept responsibility for the achievement of 90 per cent of the target to be raised from their own resources and from the statutory, other corporate and trust sectors . . . High income earners who fell outside the constituency being approached by the Fundraising Group should be covered by direct mail towards the end of the campaign period . . . for figures not less than £1,000.' The prospective chairman was a highly motivated businessman who lived in the area. The Development Corporation expressed 'quiet confidence that both leadership and the size of gift required will be forthcoming' if he were to take the lead.

He did take the chair. The appeal delivered its target, and the Alzheimer's Centre opened. It is now fully functioning.

Creating a new university

The programme to create a new University of Lincolnshire had remarkable origins. The great Cathedral City of Lincoln had never had its own university. For a short period during the thirteenth and early fourteenth centuries, rebellious scholars from Oxford established Brasenose Hall in Stamford. They duly returned to Oxford, which was then in the Lincoln diocese, and re-settled to form the Brasenose College of today. Apart from that episode, and before Grimsby was brought back into the county, Lincolnshire had never had a university of its own.

After two of its members had agreed in conversation that Lincolnshire needed a university for economic, social and cultural reasons, the CBI published this ambition in one line of its document, *Towards the Year 2000*. Elected members and the senior officers of the county council backed the project, which was strongly and practically supported by the Training and Enterprise Council (TEC).

The then Tory-led county council pledged £10 million towards creating the university and commissioned a study to develop the strategic plan for fundraising. The planning study started in March 1993, and the plan was completed in July of that year.

The planning study was to review: the financial requirements; the case for support; the sources for an appeal; medium and longer-term strategies; requirements for investment and resources; record and monitoring systems; structures and procedures for consolidation. About 50 interviews were carried out by the consultants with key individuals, and there were many more meetings. All successful appeals depend on people, and this was vividly the case in Lincolnshire. The success of the whole enterprise at critical moments depended on five or six people from the appeal leadership, the TEC, the county's education department and the county council itself.

There were some clear principles on which this university's appeal had to be built. Although it was to be a national institution it was starting as a University for Lincolnshire; and, although it was a university for all of Lincolnshire, it was opening in Lincoln, where the campus was to be sited (a decision reached late during the planning study). The original intention was that places remote from Lincoln would be served through learning and teaching centres, electronically linked to the main campus. Although the appeal would eventually reach out to national sources beyond Lincolnshire, its first phase would be confined within the county. The report stated: 'If Lincolnshire is to create its university, the people of Lincolnshire must demonstrate they want it'.

Given that premise, the major support aspect of the appeal's first phase had to concentrate on very few sources and call on them for sums well beyond anything sought from them before within the county. This was Lincoln's biggest enterprise since the building of its cathedral. The estimated capital requirement for establishing the university was £32 million, although some of those interviewed believed the costs would rise to £50 million. This was the sum on which the unit targets projected were based. A fairly recent appeal for Lincoln's City Technology College had raised about £300,000 'with some pain'. The highest unit contributions to that from companies had been around £25,000. Now unit targets were being set of £10 million (one, already committed), £5 million (one), £3 million (one), £1 million (five), £500,000 (seven), £250,000 (ten), £100,000 (twenty five). This presupposed at least 150 to 200 good prospective sources. The report warned: 'If there are not sufficient sums about, say, £1 million the pressure downwards will become impossible' and 'if units of support (achieved) cluster below £200,000 . . . the feasibility of the university project is in doubt, unless there are known external sources to compensate for this.'

There was consequent heavy pressure on the sources identified as prospects for phase one. Of course, for the phase of the appeal which had such local emphasis, many of the main corporate sources were known and already involved. These included the programme's instigators. Some main private sources emerged from the ordinary processes of the appeal's first stage. A woman came up at a press reception to say that she and her husband had a trust they were going to wind up (by then they knew the scale of funding needed) and said they would like to back the university. They eventually gave about £250,000. Generally, however, identification of prospects with their targeting was achieved through formal research.

Sources included the city council and other local authorities. Some were disappointed because the campus was located in Lincoln, yet they came through with substantial sums, the highest being £1 million. The TEC continued its support, and members of the CBI and the Chamber of Commerce were to be canvassed individually, with endorsement from the umbrella bodies. This meant that information had to be gathered very discretely, since the programme was taking place inside a very close community. There were also a few national groups and the regional utilities that had to be profiled and engaged. An external research agency was brought in to review wealth within the county and early national sources outside it. Negotiation through the original academic partner, Nottingham Trent, continued with national government and particularly the Higher Education Funding Council for England.

Some prospects had convinced themselves of the basic validity of the case for a university before its appeal began. But not all conclusions are as easy as that. It had to be shown how the university would serve all the county. As discussions began the detail was still unclear. For example, how would a remote learning and teaching centre be operated? Who would be there? Would there be tutorials? What technology would be employed? Who would have access? These questions were being asked by some of the main early prospects. Soon the questions shifted: how would the university serve the interests of this utility or the interests of the food industry in the south of the county? Other questions were more general. A group that gave over £1.5 million had said that it would not be a significant user of graduates or of academic research but it wanted to be convinced the university would be a factor for strengthening the local economy and it needed arguments and figures to prove this to its board. A more difficult question was how to prevent the university from excessive political influence, given the crucial role of the county council in its foundation.

There were also crucial communications issues to be addressed by the plan. This was a project for the whole of the county but it was to have its main campus in Lincoln. The early initiative for it had been taken from Lincoln. Yet everyone had to be and feel involved and have a sense of ownership of their university. An expert communication team was introduced. It was important that there should be no premature messages that would attract inadequate levels of

CHAPTER SIX **VARIABLE STRATEGIES**

response from major prospects not yet close to the programme; but, given the nature of the programme, it was impossible and undesirable that the programme be kept secret. There were too many institutions, groups and people to be briefed and consulted for there to be secrets. Also, from a fairly early moment, a broad popular movement had to be mobilised behind the project. It was an early finding of the study that there were 'individuals, groups, sections of the county whose partnership and support will affect success of the project but who have until now felt (and been) excluded from participation and from communication about the project'.

The strategic plan described a long-term structure for voluntary funding which, recognising the board's inalienable responsibilities, included a president with vice-presidents and a court which would offer 'a place where funders can be specially acknowledged and where potent non-funders can be associated at a senior level with the programme', but without powers or authority. More crucially, it was proposed that there should be a foundation, as at Cambridge, responsible for funding development and for raising and disbursing funds for objects and within policies as defined by the board at any time. 'There would be exchanges on policy and priorities between board and foundation, but without compromising the board's integrity.' Such an arrangement has the potential to be hugely productive, and it was proposed here to reduce, but not remove, political influence: the council would have had *ex-officio* representation on the foundation, which would have been chaired from outside the board. However, this part of the plan was not accepted. The politics would in any case be contained as the university, with its distinct autonomy, came into its own.

This is an account of the strategy for Lincolnshire, not of its implementation (for which systems and procedures had been recommended). Levels of support had been proposed and warnings given on the consequences of not achieving their higher segments. The £10 million pledge by the county council was a main determinant which, despite the doubts expressed by some respondents to the study, never wavered. The Tories initiated this, but Labour, in conjunction with the Liberal Democrats, saw it through. The commitments that followed were now crucial. The people involved did not run great national companies and had never given before at the levels proposed. When the man selected as chairman of the appeal was told by the fundraisers that a pledge of £500,000 was needed from one of the close sources, he said 'I suppose it must be me.' He then took another close source, already verbally committed to £100,000, out to dinner with the principal university and county council people, and said what he was doing. The challenge was taken up, and a new £500,000 pledged. These were not the richest sources, but they had set markers well above £200,000. The strategy was viable.

During the study the senior officer within the education department whose vision and activity were among the factors which made this project succeed said that 'unanimous backing for the University for Lincolnshire was *achieved*'. It did not come about by accident. Short accounts of great enterprises can make everything sound easy. The funding for this new university was achieved because people, companies, organisations and communities wanted the university, believed in it and had the commitment to see it through. National government did not support the capital programme but finally had to support the early functioning of this new university, which will be important to region and nation. The new university opened in the autumn of 1996. The strategy for voluntary fundraising and its implementation were vital for this.

Complexities

There are complexities of all kinds to be dealt with in the design and implementation of strategies, even for quite conventional and well-resourced organisations. There are also danger signals which may show during the study. It may be difficult to interpret the signs that principal trustees and senior management are simply gesturing when they say they are committed to a programme's success. Where the team responsible for action and the leadership have been able and determined to make the programme succeed, targets can be achieved despite such negativity. In other instances, the board's directorate has been known to look on, carping, as the fundraising team was left to wallow. Everybody in the organisation – especially those at the top – must have the will as well as the desire to succeed. Everyone wants money, but it takes will and work to win it.

Confronting public perceptions

The plan must be designed in terms of the realities as they are known or perceived. An organisation may achieve high awareness ratings in the quantitative surveys but operate in a field which lacks universal appeal. Rationality is a significant factor in fundraising, and causes are valued very differently, irrespective of their intrinsic worth. Thus blindness maybe, deafness probably and mental illness certainly evoke less ready responses than children or causes relating to cancer, the prevention of cruelty to animals or animal welfare. There are greater extremes. It can be very difficult to make a convincing case to many people that help for abusers, the provision of alternatives to custody for young offenders, a de-tox and rehabilitation unit in an urban centre are causes deserving support. Of course, the greater the difficulty the stronger the argument to those who will listen. The problem becomes part of the case. But as the numbers of people who will listen are reduced, it becomes more difficult to find them. Some such appeals eventually depend on a few enlightened trusts and philanthropists.

Shelter, for example, was seen by many in the British establishment as a left-wing, radical, political body in the early years of the Thatcher government. It does indeed deal with the causes as well as the effects of homelessness and is in this way radical; but it has been even-handed between political parties. However, partly because of its internal culture but also because of the way it was perceived, Shelter had lacked significant, dependable support from companies and the rich. In order to investigate ways of changing the public perception of its activities, and to increase its funding from the corporate sector, Shelter commissioned a strategic plan at the start of the 1900s. The 1991 strategic plan recommended that Shelter's 'publicity should where necessary confront its designation as "political", which is intended as a slur. To relevant target publics it should demonstrate that attacking the causes of homelessness, describing its effects, criticising harmful policies are its responsibilities as a charity. It must be clear that Shelter does not start with any party-political prejudice.' Because the campaign was starting without the networks of influence needed to move swiftly into a major support campaign, there was a gradual approach to the recruitment of leaders. Research had identified people who might share Shelter's vision and approve of its activities, and a leader was found who used dinner parties and a reception to brief prospects. The plan was clear: 'For the period ahead it is probably best to think in terms of a number of apparently loosely structured contacts and groups, the planned outcome being high-level access to companies, professions, trusts, people of means . . . The relationship should start by being fairly informal from your new volunteers' point of view; but it must be purposeful and structured in Shelter's plans.'

There are organisations for unpopular causes. There are others which are new, or developing, which have the potential to achieve national status, regardless of their likely low popularity. Two recent studies for London-based medical charities, each with a successful early track record, concluded that they had the authority and opportunity to grow into institutes with national scope and international status, thereby improving research and medical care. There were challenging financial implications for the funding of chairs, their research support, teaching, training, the dissemination of information as well as the delivery of services. The organisations were in different fields. Both had medical specialists and lay development staff who were devoted to the cause of improving understanding and provision for the people they served. There were strategic plans that recommended that each should re-establish itself as a national institute in its field. This demanded daunting decisions from the trustees and directorates. There are no guarantees of success; no avoidance of risk.

The Northern Ireland Voluntary Trust: overcoming unpopularity

Similarly daunting decisions faced the Northern Ireland Voluntary Trust (NIVT), when, in 1980, its trustees decided how they would match a conditional grant of £250,000 from government through voluntary funding (there is a published account of this initiative in Mullin, 1995: this section simply notes key points concerning the strategy and early leadership, which eventually secured the trust's now remarkable success). NIVT was formed because there was a scarcity of trust funding in Northern Ireland and because grants from Britain into community and cross-community projects in Northern Ireland were often hijacked by the extremists or misdirected, thereby exacerbating sectarian division.

The strategy had to accommodate three facts at the start of the initiative: generally, people in Britain preferred to disown the crisis in Northern Ireland or considered proposed remedies hopeless; the trust did not yet effectively exist, although it had been formed with trustees expert in the province's community affairs; the appeal lacked leadership, since the trustees had, with one exception, been selected for their knowledge of the situations within and between communities, not for their fundraising clout. A further fact about voluntary funding into Northern Ireland was that most decisions about substantial sums were taken in London.

The strategy had to allow for these facts. In order to give itself a track record, the trust needed to fund early projects out of its statutory endowment, replacing this as income from an appeal began to come in. The appeal itself had to be centred in London, where the decisions on major funding were made, not in Belfast or Derry. The case had to show that there was a need for this initiative and that it had good prospects for improving cross-community relations in Northern

Ireland. Those points were easily established. The difficulty was to enlist fundraising leadership for the project.

The plan made it clear that the programme could only succeed if it could command attention from main London-based decision makers and reach them personally. It took more than eighteen months before, through Jane Ewart-Biggs's involvement and persuasion, a leadership team was formed around Sir Fred Catherwood, with Sir David Orr (then chairman of Unilever), Lord Carr, Sir Brian Corby (chairman of Prudential), Sir Campbell Adamson (chairman of Abbey National), and Nicholas Horsley (chairman of Northern Foods) as members. The prospects for leadership had been identified through research undertaken to find people resident in Britain who had strong links with Northern Ireland, either through birth, education or corporate interests. The chairman and first director of the trust were further crucial aspects of NIVT's leadership, and without their belief in the strategy and commitment to it – they had been partners in its design – the programme would have failed. The programme, which at its inception was highly risky, has now exceeded its targets, in terms of the capital base established and the throughput of funds.

Change and competition

There are always external factors which affect the realisation of a strategy, and to which the fund-raising *strategos* must respond. Changes in the economy affected the achievement of some major appeals in the late 1980s and early 1990s or made it necessary to protract an appeal if it was to achieve its result. Over the same period, as competition increased, organisations had to work harder and with greater ingenuity to find and enlist fundraising leaders. Government policies change. For example, a continuing fundraising campaign for the Integrated Education movement in Northern Ireland – which was based on the idea that there should be a 60 : 40 ratio between the main denominations among pupils, teachers and governors – ran into difficulties when the Northern Ireland Office changed its criteria for identifying an integrated school. This shift jeopardised the statutory funding of those schools that continued to try to match the original criteria. Vagaries in university funding have created special problems. In one instance, while a museum attached to one of the new universities was securing £1.6 million from the Heritage Lottery Fund, cuts in funding were forcing the Vice Chancellor to close down courses in art and design. Demonstrations and protests in the press from public figures caused the university to reconsider its support for the museum, which had been a condition of the lottery grant. At Lincoln, the Higher Education Funding Council for England decided to offer funding for a number of students below the level at which the new university would be viable. A swift and radical renegotiation of the new university's academic partnerships was needed to save the project. By contrast, a transfer of political power within the county had not detrimentally affected the university's fundraising.

An appeal may also be ambushed, either accidentally or deliberately. There is active warfare over regular supporters, for example, between two Christian relief agencies, the one representing itself as the modern, ecumenical alternative to its Catholic rival, which is presented by implication as old-fashioned, traditional and narrowly sectarian. In another case, as we have seen, the less popular of two rival agencies operating in the same, difficult field was beginning to build its leadership, with patchy and unenthusiastic help from its board. It was suddenly found that the rival agency was launching a major appeal against the same target segment, and already had its leadership in place. The less popular agency decided to postpone its initiative.

Internal, operational and organisational problems

A strategy may also be wrecked from within. This will happen if implementation is undertaken lackadaisically, with no commitment of the energy needed to engender the increasing returns a great total strategy demands. Well-researched appeals chairs, heads of major companies, can also fail. In two such instances, the first had gone behind his company's public affairs committee and produced £150,000 for the cause, the second gave nothing. Both promised contacts and action at meetings but did nothing between them. Neither chivvied their committees into action. The meetings became stereotyped and static, and there was a real danger of support dropping away. Both men were confronted with the fact that their inaction was costing the cause, and people served, millions of pounds. They still did nothing, but not out of malice – one through lethargy, the other because, as he eventually revealed, he did not believe in the strategy. The steering committee, consisting of the treasurer, the finance director, the consultant and, critically, a senior banker, effectively took over the latter appeal and, with great effort, brought it through to a good if expensively achieved result. The other appeal also limped through to a kind of success. Finally, there was the famous 'Make Children Happy' disaster, which left many small charities with their expectations unmet. Its launch publicity was so successful that everyone noted its collapse. What was the reason for this? It based its expectations on a single source: Ladbroke's pioneering lottery.

Some threatening situations arise from an organisation's operations. When Marie Colwell died, NSPCC shared the blame for her death and addressed the matter directly with their supporters. They were open and honest about their failure and what they would do about it. This was a deliberate decision which had the incidental effect of engendering increased income. Another organisation found, as the strategy for fundraising was being developed, that it was about to be hit by a massive deficit. There needed to be action before any longer-term strategy could be introduced. They decided to take regular supporters into their confidence through an emergency appeal, based on a letter from the director. Roughly half of those mailed responded positively, substantially reducing the deficit. The fact that 50 per cent of supporters did respond, and 50 per cent did not, suggested a difference between the two segments which could be used in future communications.

Finally, the plan may aim to demonstrate that a particular methodology is feasible for it. A leading charity in one of the Scandinavian countries did not believe major support fundraising was possible in that country. The fundraising records certainly showed no sign of major support received – but none had been sought. It was found that all gifts above a certain size were acknowledged by the Secretary General and never entered the fundraising records. An interview with the head of one of the country's main manufacturers revealed that companies in that country had supported educational, and some other causes at high levels. When asked what made a company give substantial sums, the chairman pointed to the wall, behind which sat the country's senior banker and one of its grandest, richest men: 'Where he goes we follow,' he said.

The strategic plan hopes to foresee main problems and possible disasters, so as to prevent or avoid them. However, information can never be complete and no plan, however thoroughly prepared, can protect the organisation or its fundraising from external shocks and changes in circumstances. The people who implement such strategies must therefore be alert, resourceful, robust, flexible, creative and opportunistic, if they are to deal effectively with the unpredictable.

CHAPTER SEVEN

Experiences of strategies

A single voice has been heard to this point. In this chapter, a series of people speak who think strategically, who have worked within, and helped define, strategies. Some also comment on the problems of winning co-operation and support in designing strategies and carrying them through. Here there is statement of fallibility in the best strategic planning; and of waverings in its implementation.

Strategies for schools

The concept of a long-term fundraising and development strategy is relatively new in British schools* although it has been embraced by most American private schools for at least 20, and in many cases more than 30, years. This is principally because the idea of a 'development culture', one which nurtures past, present and potential donors and develops in them a sense of involvement and ownership in the school in question is one which has yet to take root here, though not for want of trying. Measured against our American cousins, British schools are, in this respect at least, mired in the Dark Ages. The simple, if disappointing, truth is that many governors and heads take the 'hit and run' approach to fundraising: take notice of alumni and parents when you want their voluntary financial support, wing out a brief series of thank-you letters and progress reports in the immediate aftermath of a fundraising campaign, and then forget about them until the next one. Interestingly many of the instances of poor or unsuccessful practice have issued from a misapprehension of what actually happens in the United States.

---

* Although, increasingly, schools in the maintained sector are developing fundraising activities to supplement scant resources, this chapter focuses on the independent sector. Where the word 'school' is used, therefore, the implication is that, unless otherwise stated, this is a private, or independent, school.

Five instances of poor practice

Many heads and governors still hold the view that a continuous rolling campaign is bound to generate more funds and be less trouble administratively than periodic campaigns every seven years or so (this was the traditional model – the main perceived weakness of which was that it 'missed out' on several years of parents each time). While a rolling campaign may start well, the fact that people can see no clear end in sight means that gradually the focus becomes blurred, commitment and enthusiasm wane (both of those actively involved in the leadership of the campaign and of potential donors), and it eventually grinds to a halt. By that stage, all potential donors have been approached and therefore 'vaccinated' against further giving, and a significant fallow period of several years is needed before any active fundraising initiatives can be attempted.

There is also the temptation to go for a massive target, based on the false premises that (a) it will excite massive support and (b), given a long enough time span, it will be achievable even where the true potential is very much smaller. What actually tends to happen is that the target is never seen as credible by potential donors, who take fright and withdraw altogether, not wanting to be associated with failure. The campaign eventually peters out after four or five years with a sum far short of the target and a palpable air of failed expectations.

Equally demotivating is the concept of asking donors to contribute to a central 'pot' (for example, a 'Development Fund') with no detail of the needs on which it is to be spent, the justification for them or details of the costings. Donors expect and deserve accountability and, if they do not perceive it, they will not give. Unfortunately, by the time schools discover their mistake, it is often too late for them drastically to change direction without damaging, often terminally, the credibility of the enterprise.

Then there is the 'If everyone gave X' approach. The division of a target sum by the number of potential donors to arrive at an average contribution ignores two simple facts. First, not everyone will give. Secondly, disposable income varies enormously and to set an average level allows those who could give substantially more to get off very lightly, while it probably deters those who cannot afford the suggested level from giving at all. Bear in mind that in most successful campaigns – not just school campaigns – between 35 per cent and 50 per cent of the gross total is likely to come from fewer than 20 gifts.

Finally, many governing bodies and some bursars still presume that one of the prime laws of commerce – that a satisfactory return or yield requires an adequate level of investment – does not apply when it comes to fundraising. It is astounding that astute, highly successful businessmen and women who would consider a return of 10 or 15 per cent on their capital to be satisfactory (as indeed it is) question a *cost level* of between 10 and 15 per cent when it comes to fundraising – or, to put it the other way round, returns of 500 to 600 per cent.

Cultivating alumni

There is however, plenty of good news. The message is finally beginning to take root, at least among a small number of forward-thinking schools, that fundraising is in simple terms a practical manifestation of goodwill towards an institution. In order to keep funds coming in, therefore, it is necessary to ensure that the reservoir of goodwill remains topped up – thus moving the emphasis from solicitation to cultivation. This is an essential first step in establishing a cost-effective and sustainable development structure.

One or two schools, after successful capital campaigns, are investing considerable time and effort in cultivating their alumni. One major independent school has taken the bold step of undertaking a detailed communications audit on the premise that, if you find out what parents and alumni *really* think of you and how comprehensive and effective your communications with them are, you can begin the process of creating a genuine mutually beneficial relationship (a partnership of involvement) responding to their needs and requirements and enabling you to correct misconceptions. Such an approach, if properly implemented and sustained, is bound to result in a marked increase in goodwill which will have an impact not just on fundraising but on pupil recruitment. This is indeed proving to be the case at the school in question.

Continuing neglect of fundraising potential

Fundraising is still regarded by many independent schools as an occasional peripheral activity, but it is becoming an increasingly important part of the funding mix, the other components of which, broadly speaking, are fee income and income from other activities. Keen ornithologists or photographers will know that a bipod will give you a degree of stability but if you want a really steady platform you need a tripod (to misquote Orwell, 'two legs shaky, three legs better'). The same applies when it comes to funding: the three parts of the funding mix – the tripod's legs – are not all equal in financial terms, but they all have a significant part to play in maximising funding potential. Most independent schools, one hopes, will be pretty good at optimising fee income and other income-generating activities such as facilities lettings. However, there is still a considerable number – if not the majority – that regards voluntary funding at best as a retractable leg which goes down periodically when additional support is needed (the classic periodic capital campaign every seven years with absolutely no activity in-between), at worst as a suspect and undesirable third leg, the mere use of which suggests that a school is teetering on the brink of a precipice – by which time it is probably not going to help anyway.

Yet this is probably the area where there is the greatest room for growth. Fee income is limited principally by two factors: the number of pupils you can take and the market rates for the education you are providing. Similarly, use of facilities for additional revenue generation is governed by the size and nature of those facilities, the periods for which they are available for letting out and, again, the market rates you can charge. Of course there are limits to voluntary funding, but few schools have genuinely reached that limit.

The pressures on funding for schools, especially independent schools, have increased significantly over recent years, and there is general consensus that they will continue to increase rather than lessen. That being the case, schools would be well advised to take voluntary fundraising seriously.

Mark Jefferies
Director of Schools Fundraising, Craigmyle and Company Ltd

Some reflections on practical issues concerning the implementation of a total strategy

All systems go?

So you have your new strategy? You've been to the conferences; read Mullin, Burnett and Nichols; consulted your managers endlessly. Finally, your shiny, sophisticated strategy has been unanimously passed by the trustees. Your problems are over.

No. Your problems are just about to start.

Segmentation

Your strategy, unless it is one of total anarchy, will almost certainly have involved segmenting the potential market in some way: by activity, or type of donor, or both. As a result, donors will have been put into boxes.

Any such segmentation is merely a construct. It may look wonderful on paper, but it is essentially an attempt to apply order into a world that simply isn't ordered. The woman who chairs your committee in one place may be married to the managing director of a company you are working with in another. The millionaire philanthropist who gives £15 occasionally does so because that's all he is asked to do. He was first recruited via a direct mail appeal. And the major supporter who is so moved by one of your television commercials suddenly becomes a 'TV donor'.

Ownership

Once donors have been put into boxes, the likelihood is that dealing with them becomes the particular responsibility of one department, or fundraiser. Because that fundraiser has targets to meet, a sense of territorial ownership develops. Rather than taking an organisation-wide view, thinking tends to revolve around how income from donors can be maximised within their existing boxes. The tendency will therefore be that donors will be handled by the department that first brought them in, rather than where they might be best handled for the good of the organisation.

Measurement

How do you break out of this situation? Increasingly, the essence of successful fundraising is based upon relationships. The world of commerce is becoming 'customer oriented', in the same way as we are becoming 'donor led'. We are putting the donor at the centre of the picture, thinking about *their* needs and *their* timescale.

However, although your trustees probably thought your idea of building long-term relationships with donors was excellent, they then want you to set annual income targets – against which you are judged. The idea of long-term relationships is wonderful, but the measurements of success, donor satisfaction and so on are pretty intangible. On the other hand, money in the bank is so, so tangible, and money is what is needed to enable the organisation to survive. So the organisation will be committed to a long-term view of fundraising, but will go into spasms the first month the results are seriously down. In turn, this must rub off on fundraising staff who forego all strategic thought in order to get cash in.

Disownership

A number of problems arise out of this: if you are not my donor, then I haven't got time to do anything for you. Donors neither understand nor care for the internal structures of our organisation. They simply want their money to go to the cause. And yet, how many times does a donor with a small query get transferred from one department to another to another before finally giving up in exasperation?

Donor expectations

This brings me to another point. The expectations donors have of the charities they support are completely different from the expectations they have of the companies from whom they purchase. If a donor buys something for £15 from a company, they do so because they think it's worth £15 to them. They don't really care if the company wastes money, sends out unnecessary junk mail or has large amounts of cash in its reserves. However, a donor giving £15 to a charity has a completely different mind-set. If you send them too many letters, you are wasting money of theirs that could have gone to help the beneficiaries; money spent on 'administration' is money that should be going to the cause. At the same time, their expectations of the efficiency of charities and companies are also radically different. 'Allow 28 days for delivery' is acceptable when ordering goods by mail order, but 'allow 28 days for your receipt' has them reaching for paper and envelope.

They expect you to remember the letter they sent in 1979, in which they asked you not to send the Christmas catalogue. If you write to

Mrs M Peters at her new address in Basingstoke, she expects you to remember that she is the same M Peters who once chaired a committee in Middlesbrough. You have 300 M Peters on your database: how could you possibly know? The Duke of Dorset regales you about the expensive, highly-personalised letter he received with a typed-in 'Dear Duke of Dorset', ostensibly hand-signed by one of his peers. 'I phoned him up the moment I got it and asked him why he didn't mention it over dinner the previous night!'

Failure to meet these donor expectations, despite the tens of thousands of donations and warm letters that flood in as a result of your appeal, leads to the arrival of hundreds of complaining letters on the chief executive's desk, many of them highly articulate, heart-rending and all needing careful handling. The chief executive is not amused.

New money versus old money

If there is one thing your donors *do* like, it is raising money for some brand new project that isn't going to see the light of day unless they help to fund it. Your colleagues on the other side of the organisation love it too; they want to get their hands on these new projects so that they can do more good for the beneficiaries. And your fundraising staff love 'new' projects because they are exciting, and so much easier to raise money for. So who raises the millions that are needed year in, year out simply to keep the organisation going? Somehow that money is just supposed to come in.

Conclusion

So your strategy is coming unstuck left, right and centre. The social-work staff don't like you because you won't let them have their new projects. Your own staff are too busy squabbling over who gets allocated the £10,000 cheque that's just come in. Your chief executive doesn't like you because you've upset all these donors that he now has to placate. Whom do you turn to? The trustees? No, their main concern is the design of the Christmas cards, and the fact that you won't let the volunteers have goods for their fete on sale or return.

So before you judge the brilliance of your written strategy, don't forget that, as Thomas Edison might have said, a successful strategy is one per cent inspiration and ninety nine per cent implementation.

Giles Pegram
Appeals Director and Deputy Chief Executive, NSPCC

Developing a total strategy

Initial assumptions

In order to place the development of a total fundraising strategy in context it is necessary at the outset to state two key assumptions that affect much of the subsequent thinking. First, that the organisation will in parallel produce a credible, all-encompassing case for support which reaches or appeals to – in the broadest sense – all sections of the national (and possibly international) community. Secondly, that a comprehensive campaign is required, involving a range of needs or services and thereby making a diversity of sources applicable, as opposed to a highly targeted initiative around a more limited response.

These may appear obvious assumptions but they have a direct bearing on both the stages of communication required to generate momentum in a controlled fashion and also on who should be involved in developing the fundraising strategy. Depending on the organisational context, it may be possible to have a wide, all-encompassing process from the outset. On the other hand, as was the case at NSPCC (see page 95 for earlier comment on this total campaign), it was necessary to inform, educate and involve constituents at different times and in different ways (for example, trustees, staff, donors and potential leadership figures).

Establishing the framework for research

Having set out with some initial assumptions our next stage was to establish certain key questions that the strategy would seek to answer:

- Taking the demonstrated, and costed, need, could we identify sufficient numbers of prospects to meet this goal? What was the availability of wealth in the given constituency?

- Could we identify routes of contact to access these prospects? How many of these prospects were known to be philanthropic?

- Could we identify and mobilise the required levels of voluntary leadership to use these networks?

- Could we define an organisational strategy and structure that is likely to be successful in this context?

This last point posed an interesting point of sequence. Classic fundraising theory implies that the strategy should be developed after the likely sources of support have been identified. However, our strategy was also likely to include some hypotheses which would require research or testing, for example the development of certain fundraising sub-strategies or products in particular sections of the overall universe of possible support.

An interim strategy was therefore required which would lay down an analysis of potential markets and methodologies and could be used as the basis for informing research or a programme of testing. For example, where methodologies were deemed to be proven, either within the context of NSPCC or elsewhere, no testing would be carried out. However, where assumptions had been made in producing the interim strategy which were unproven, then these would be 'tested' as far as practicable.

It is worth bearing in mind at this point that the fundraising strategy would ultimately need to gain the assent of both trustees and initial voluntary leaders. Consequently the demonstration of feasibility against certain propositions was both for 'real' and 'persuasive' purposes.

The need for communication

Conversely an important point was stressed in the strategy. Although our research would seek to demonstrate that wealth existed in sufficient quantities to meet our targets, and that the organisation could identify and secure initial interest from the types of major philanthropists likely to support such an initiative, this in no way should be taken as proof of future success. Indeed, we were clear that, although the levels of gift we were assuming throughout the intended programme had been delivered individually elsewhere, they had never before been secured to a single campaign by a British charitable welfare institution. In an organisation with varying levels of knowledge this needed careful communication, particularly as we wished to stress the point that ultimately success would depend on both the power of our voluntary leadership and our organisational focus and commitment.

This point is also valid when attempting to draw comparisons between organisations. The nature, scale and methodologies of any proposed campaign will inevitably be determined by the organisational context within which it is developed. NSPCC already operated major fundraising and also had existing voluntary leadership structures. As such the campaign was being planned from a different base, with accompanying advantages and disadvantages, to, say, a new charity or organisation starting from a low or zero base.

Prospect management

Our key area of consideration when formulating a major appeal strategy alongside existing fundraising operations was that of prospect control. How do you accommodate the varying needs of protecting on-going income, the wishes of your existing volunteers to use their contacts for this year's activity and the recognition that many of your major campaign gifts will come from those supporters already known to you? An interesting tension exists between the organisation's ability to 'control' its volunteers on one hand, and 'anarchy' on the other, in the sense that powerful supporters will inevitably speak to whom they like, when they like. Equally, will donors support on-going fundraising from annual income, while making major campaign gifts from assets, or is there a danger of 'vaccination', with donors feeling they have already given to your cause – even if the level is too low for your campaign needs?

The solutions to these questions will be determined differently by different organisations. At NSPCC, a system was developed to review all major donors or prospects monthly and to have parallel tracks whereby on-going fundraising progressed alongside campaign structures, with supporters selecting their preferred involvement at an appropriate time. The level of resource on prospect research was also significantly enhanced.

NSPCC's normal method of understanding the potential universe of support is via market segmentation: approaching prospects according to whether they are an individual donor, a company, a foundation or trust. In the context of a major campaign strategy this posed several interesting dilemmas. For example, how do you separate the needs and wishes of a major individual from the giving preferences of their foundation, or their position at the head of a top corporate prospect?

Equally, are some individuals so wealthy or global in their outlook that they can only be involved in a unique way with others of equal status? Where in your strategy, if you are in a devolved organisation, do you place extremely wealthy individuals (national prospects) who happen to live outside London, and have loyalties to the place where they live? Do donors who have acquired significant wealth more recently represent better gift prospects than apparently wealthier families whose assets are part of an inherited estate? The actual sources and methods of using these sources will clearly need to be developed at the appropriate time during the campaign, according to the needs of the donor, the appeal and the preference of the campaign leadership.

Answering these questions, and producing the final strategy, will involve an assessment of the individual needs (and likely philanthropy) of each individual likely to be able, or willing, to make a major campaign gift. These individual needs will then have to be placed in a context where the donors will donate at the right time with the right people to the right part of the cause.

Monitoring and evaluation

Having embarked on the actual process of fundraising it is essential to build in a process for review. It is critical: to define benchmarks or milestones by when certain key objectives should be reached and to ensure relevant stakeholders – the fundraising leadership, trustees of the organisation, staff and do on, all agree the measures and timetable for evaluation.

The benchmarks developed can and should reflect all elements of the fundraising process. In addition to the bare analysis of cash income received and additional pledges made, it may also be necessary to analyse how the case for support or organisation's mission has been received. Can it be refined? Do you need to communicate how effective the organisation's use of early monies raised has been? In the NSPCC's case it has been essential to show how new projects and services made possible by FULL STOP have begun to impact on the goal of ending cruelty to children, in order to seek second (or more) gifts from early donors, approach new prospects or go back to others unreceptive to previous solicitations.

This process will call into question the information systems of the organisation. How many of the originally identified possible donors have been approached? Did they give, and if so at or below expectations? If approaches failed, can you establish why – not only to learn for the next phase of your campaign but also because critical parts of your message may be being lost or concerns (or perceptions) of the organisation may be held which need addressing?

In developing a total strategy it is likely that some elements will perform better than others. Achievements against different parts of the scheduled gift table may vary, or different elements of the leadership structure or fundraising 'products' will perform more or less well. This has two key implications.

Firstly, your analysis will be a useful tool in testing certain assumptions made early in the campaign, and should influence future strategy. Secondly, and perhaps crucially to the organisation, varying returns in both time and scale may affect the implementation of the organisation's mission. Tactical decisions may be needed both on implementation of services and also the future scale and resourcing of the fundraising campaign.

In the case of the NSPCC certain parts of the strategy proved highly successful, particularly when implemented in tandem with high-profile media and communication messages. Equally, the strong existing volunteer network allowed for the development of a powerful board and extensive series of sub-groupings by industry sector, sport, region, etc. Where progress was more difficult was in achieving gifts at the highest end of the required table, i.e. £5 million plus.

A goal of ending child cruelty can inspire with its vision but also seem nebulous against more traditional, non-social service causes such as universities. Perhaps most crucially the campaign began without enough gifts at this level from within the appeal leadership itself. Outstanding gifts were achieved at lower levels and particularly in the mid range, perhaps £100,000–£1 million. However, to achieve the overall goal, higher figures are crucial and a key element of the review process has been to redefine a more project-based case for support to strengthen the element of tangibility, and to secure additional leadership willing to give and ask for other gifts at the higher pace-setting levels.

A sensitive area in any process of review will be evaluating the performance of the appeal leadership. Have members of the board met the critical tests of commitment to the task and organisation, making or delivering gifts from themselves, their family or organisation, and then asking for and securing gifts from others?

An early element of the strategy will be to ensure the board owns and adopts the case for support, the requirement for funds it sets out and the process and timetable for delivery of these funds. A most likely cause of failure against agreed benchmarks may be ineffective leadership or an inability to transfer fully the ownership and responsibility for the appeal to those required to deliver it.

Equally, a diverse board of volunteers will bring a range of skills and contacts, as well as motivations. Some will be genuinely philanthropic or may need to link directly to the cause; others will be seeking social recognition or some form of mutual benefit or payback. A few may display some or all of these in tandem. As the campaign progresses and a review process is implemented it may be necessary to acknowledge different needs for recognition or communication, private, public, social and so on.

Finally, any campaign will be subject to outside factors, perhaps combining elements of both private and public support. These are often outside the control of the organisation – economy, world affairs, etc. But in setting the campaign timetable it is important to review when certain critical elements are required, their sensitivity or susceptibility to outside influence and the impact of this on other factors within the appeal.

Nick Booth
Campaign Director, NSPCC FULL STOP campaign

Prospect research in the development and implementation of a fundraising strategy

The role of research

Does research play a part in the development and implementation of a fundraising strategy?

Why ask? Pose this question in a business rather than a 'charity' setting, and the answer is obvious.

An organisation is about to raise, or spend, millions of pounds. Should we focus our resources here, or there? Should we devise fundraising products like this, or like that? Whom should we sell to? How can we reduce the risks inherent in this new venture?

And you wonder why we should carry out research?

Research reduces risk and comforts worried management; it cuts costs by targeting marketing; and it provides a firm factual framework for implementing change in an organisation.

If all these features are vital in business they are even more important in the non-profit sector, which, we should remember, holds funds in trust for its donors and its clients. Non-profit must limit their exposure to risk – and the simplest way of doing so is to use research to understand what the risks, and the opportunities, are.

But this is an argument for all forms of research. What about prospect research?

Prospect research

Prospect research means the identification and characterisation of potential donors and supporters. In other words, prospect researchers tell you who will give, and why, when, what, how and where they will give.

In the development of a fundraising strategy prospect research helps management to understand their fundraising 'markets' – the people and the institutions they lead. By reviewing the key markets from which funds may be raised (people, companies, trusts and foundations and government) prospect researchers give a factual basis for the strategy.

By identifying the key motives of donors, prospect researchers help management to develop fundraising 'products', such as a legacy or a major gift programme, which satisfy those donor motives.

And researchers, sifting through the non-profit's existing donors, identify the historic gaps and weaknesses in fundraising – gaps and weaknesses that must be addressed by the strategy.

When the time comes to implement the strategy, research becomes a top priority. Simply put, research gives you the names of people who will give. Without research the strategy cannot be implemented.

But, if it is simply used to provide lists of names, research will under-perform. During implementation, well-managed research will also:

- track progress;
- instigate new fundraising products and new directions;
- provide reassurance to trustees that their non-profit organisation is being cautiously and professionally managed.

Can research contribute to a fundraising strategy? Yes, it can. Should we use it? Yes – above all, because it's wise.

Christopher Carnie
Director, The Factary

Strategic pitfalls

The potential pitfalls encountered in implementing a major new strategy can be numerous and diverse. The most significant are those that cannot be foreseen, that creep up from the most unexpected quarters, seriously hampering progress.

Let us assume that the fundraising strategy is sound and is based on the approach and methods used successfully by other organisations seeking to raise significant new funds in support of their cause. It has been reviewed and adapted to address the individual needs of the organisation and programme it seeks to support. The strategy has been communicated to all individuals concerned with its implementation at all stages of its development – these being the same individuals who had called for the development of the strategy as a means of introducing a new strand of support to fund an important development project. Their approval has been sought at each stage of development, their professional concerns addressed, and reassurance given. Their participation within the roles identified and outlined in the strategy has been agreed.

Yet, despite all this, the implementation of this strategy has limped forward.

There are two main factors here. First, the team responsible for the implementation of the strategy has not been delegated sufficient authority to lead the strategy implementation forward. The impact of this is manifold. Senior players have not consulted the strategy developers when a problem is encountered and have chosen their own 'quick-fix' solutions. These have fallen outside the strategic plan and so have created a different set of problems that in themselves take time and energy to sort out. Planning sessions are wasted until such time as the error is understood, confidence is regained and progress can be made in order to make up lost ground. Without sufficient authority it is not possible for an implementation team to prevent this sort of eventuality nor yet to lead with confidence, to give the assurance to the external players (in this case prospective supporters of the cause in question), and to maintain the interest and commitment of the donors already involved. There is no united front, there is no clarity in terms of leadership, there is little accountability. Without each of these a strategy has a limited chance of success.

Even after the problem has been sorted out and the roles and responsibilities clarified, the suspicion remains that, if this sort of thing has happened once, it could happen again – so the strategy progresses without the trust that is needed. The lack of respect permeates all levels – those in support roles have also come to believe that they can operate in isolation and without full consultation – so the strategy has become more vulnerable. It is important to understand the personalities involved, so as to be sure to be able to manage them appropriately. The people tasked with their management must be given sufficient authority – they must command the respect of their team to ensure that whim or lack of confidence does not throw the strategy off track.

The second major factor concerns the priority given to the strategy. An organisation cannot make the implementation of a strategy a priority simply by saying that this is the case. This trap has been a major problem in this strategy implementation. The strategy is presented to the external participants as the key and major programme for the organisation, but internally other issues are allowed to divert attention and resource. The fact that the individuals who commissioned the development of the strategy are informed is not enough – unless they are prepared to make the time, to dedicate the resources, to follow the timetable plan and to play the role allocated to them, the strategy will again falter and stall. Time before planning meetings will then be spent in a desperate flurry of activity in order to prove to the external participants that progress has been made – huge amounts of written materials generated, new promises made, reassurance given that all is well. Should the layers of reassurance ever be peeled back to reveal what is *actually* going on, a different picture would emerge. The scene would be one of some confusion, with some individuals involved seeking the time to focus on one key project rather than a number of others, while other players do no more than the minimum required. Real progress is slow, excuses are given, interest and momentum are lost.

It is important to look beyond the strategy itself at the environment within which it will operate, at the personality of the organisation and the individuals who will need to play their part. The whole organisation should have been reviewed, no assumptions should have been made that common sense would prevail and that the strategy would find its place alongside other priorities and projects. Indeed, no assumptions should have been made at all, and a fallback position should have been identified for every eventuality. If the true nature of the organisation and the individuals within it had been understood during planning – and had that truth been addressed within the terms of the strategy – problem solving would not have become the core activity of its implementation.

Anonymous

CHAPTER EIGHT

Conclusions and future directions

Fundraising makes possible the achievement of great ideals, the delivery of needed services. It is essential to the creation of the kind of society in which we want (and choose) to live. This imposes responsibilities on trustees, management, fundraisers and also on supporters. There are conclusions for training and continuing stimulation for all these people. There are some grave threats, for example from the EU, unless these are anticipated and countered. All this worry, directed skill and dedication are essential, because fundraising is the enabling function for our ideals.

Fundraising: the enabling function

Even great skills in planning and fundraising technique will lack direction and robustness if they are not grounded in the values of the not-for-profit sector, values that are expressed through service.

The use of the word 'sector' may be contentious. There are huge differences between an opera house, a hospital, a university, a unit for the homeless or disabled people, and a development agency. People from such organisations work within very different cultures. They may even resent the idea that they might share any kind of common experience or values. Yet there are essential principles shared by all such types of organisation which differentiate them from for-profit bodies. Their purpose is to serve people or meet objects as defined by their founding instruments, almost universally a trust deed, and by the trustees' policies as agreed at any time.

Another shared principle is that these organisations should cover the universe intended by their objects as comprehensively as possible with services of the highest excellence attainable by them. This means that the services must be sensitively responsive to the needs and be delivered in relevant and timely forms, whether they are concerned with performing operas, providing academic courses, supporting disabled people, serving the poor and homeless, or co-operating with third world communities in creating sustainable livelihoods. If there is activity that does not relate directly to these objectives it is surplus, even illicit (which is one reason why profit is not the purpose of these organisations' activities, except through any for-profit enterprises they may have established separately but in close relation with the main body).

If services are the principal concern of these organisations, funding is the main constraint on services, and on their scope and quality. In a few instances, an endowment or some other income source will meet all or most needs, and, more usually, there may be fees and grants from national or local government. Almost always, however, the organisation could not operate satisfactorily, or at all, without voluntary funds.

This identifies fundraising as a key enabling function for most not-for-profit organisations. This book has concentrated on procedures, processes and techniques, but it is the service made possible through fundraising which gives it value, not the mechanical excellence of its planning and technical delivery. These can be assumed to be excellent, not because of fundraisers' pride or reputation, but because this is a responsibility imposed by the priority of the services funded and of the people served. Fundraising's value is proportionate to the value of the causes it serves. This confirms the urgent need for fundraisers in all fields to have expert knowledge and skills in terms of strategic planning and techniques.

Fundraising and civil society

Fundraising helps ensure that we can enjoy the kind of society in which we prefer to live. The term 'civil society' has been used more frequently over the past few years, and not-for-profit organisations have vital roles in civil society. The term *societas civilis* was originally used for essentially monolithic and authoritarian regimes before its meaning altered, probably late in the seventeenth century. John Locke's *Two Treatises of Government* spoke of civil society as 'the soul that gives form, life and unity to the Commonwealth' (1690, section 212–30). Tom Paine perhaps made clearer what was meant: 'a great part of that order which reigns among mankind is not the effect of government. It has its origin in the principles of society and the natural constitution of man. It existed prior to government; and would exist if the formality of government were abolished' (1792, II.2). In his study of North America in the 1830s, Alexis de Tocqueville famously described the functionings of civil society there, commonly using the words 'associate' (with 'association') and 'combine' in his descriptions. He says that the people there: 'have thought of using the right of association continually in civil life . . . Americans of all ages, all stations in life, and all types of disposition are forever forming associations . . . In democratic countries knowledge of how to combine is the mother of all other forms of knowledge, on its progress depends that of all others; . . . In this way, by enjoyment of a dangerous liberty, the Americans learn the art of rendering the dangers of freedom less formidable.' (de Tocqueville, 1850).

An eloquent, more recent description of civil society was written by the Marxist, Antonio Gramsci. He was imprisoned by Mussolini between 1929 and 1935, a punishment that was fatal, his health collapsing. In his *Prison Notebooks* he distinguishes 'the ensemble of organisations commonly called "private"' (which he designates as 'civil society') from 'political society' or 'the state'. He writes: 'The superstructures of civil society are like the trench-systems of modern warfare. In war it would sometimes happen that a fierce artillery attack seemed to have destroyed the outer perimeter; at the moment of advance and attack the assailants would find themselves confronted by a line of defence which was still effective.' A complex superstructure of civil society resists economic, and other, crises. In the West, 'there was a proper relation between state and civil society, and when the state trembled a sturdy structure of civil society was at once revealed' (Gramsci, 1971).

Gramsci distinguished between the situations East and West: 'In the East the state was everything, civil society was primordial and gelatinous' (ibid.). This opens comparisons with more recent history. Hitler and Mussolini repressed or subverted voluntary agencies, such as the Scouts, in their territories. Russia had less to repress, as does present-day China. So people were more rapidly able to recover and exercise their freedoms in Poland, Czechoslovakia and Hungary where the functions of a civil society endured, than in Russia or Romania, where they were rudimentary.

However, there are other attitudes to civil society in the West, described by de Tocqueville as 'dangerous', which fear its freedoms and seek to modify them. French laws in the late eighteenth and early nineteenth centuries discouraged or prevented the formation of independent institutions and confiscated their property, following the doctrine that institutions that are not directly of and by the state should operate only within policies defined by the state. This is very different from the independence assumed for voluntary bodies within the Anglo-Saxon tradition. The argument has continued into more recent times. Foucault, reflecting Marx, argued that groups

formed as a function of civil society can impose the values and interests of powerful minorities on society, against the interests of disadvantaged minorities or the voiceless (see Cohen and Arato, 1994).

Those criticisms lack understanding of the checks and balances
between governments and voluntary agencies in the UK, North America, Australia, New Zealand and South Africa, for example. By supporting not-for-profit activity, fundraising makes a statement about
the kind of regime its supporters prefer, one in which an agency can
deliver alternative services, challenge, criticise or co-operate with
national and local governments, but always remain independent from
them. Independence of action, if it is to be secure, entails some degree
of independent funding. De Tocqueville confirms this: 'One cannot
take part in most civil associations without risking some of one's property' (1850). This gives fundraising a central role in a democracy.

Fundraising: responsibilities and challenge

If that thesis is even approximately right, fundraisers have very serious responsibilities, and the strategic planning function is vital. This
is a moment to re-examine what fundraising strategy is about and
what it achieves.

Fundraising starts with an organisation which has stated objects and
may have policies which meet these successfully in the world today. It
may lack such policies, but its objects will be clear, however vaguely
they are recalled, and it is in these that the organisation's realisable
ideals are to be found. It may well be fundraising which will make it
possible to realise them, but the strategic planning does not start
with concern about the funds, but with the vision, mission and
programme. If these are clear and costed, planning may go at once to
the next stage. If they are not clear, planning starts, excitingly and
challengingly, with a re-examination of what the organisation should
and could be doing, with vision glowing and proposed programmes
thoroughly refurbished.

The next stage of planning is to set targets and sub-targets, and to
identify the funding partners (private individuals, representatives
from companies or trusts or all of these combined) who could deliver
the funds needed. Research will deepen understanding of these
people and map networks through which to reach them. The selection of techniques and design of a timetable for the appeal will show
how and when to persuade them and will determine the resources,
organisation, monitoring and record systems required to deliver and
manage the programme. The consolidation programme will see how
relations may be sustained and developed for the future, for the

benefit of the organisation and its backers. At the core of all those exercises is a single aim: to share the ideas and idealism of the organisation with its funding partners, with mutual rewards, in a common cause.

Assuming responsibility

If a fundraising strategy concerns the organisation profoundly and touches the whole community, however defined, as a function of civil society, then what right and what competencies do the people involved in the design and realisation of the strategy (the patrons, presidents, trustees, management, staff, key volunteers and consultants) have to undertake such enterprises? There needs to be a shift from idealism to realism. Dame Janet Baker rhetorically asked how she or Bernstein or Barbirolli (and by implication the players) could dare to perform the works of the great composers. She replied they had 'the right to assume responsibility' for them because of their inwardly known and outwardly acknowledged competence to do so. How many fundraisers can legitimately affirm such a 'right to assume responsibility'?

Key considerations concerning personnel

Patrons, presidents and vice-presidents

In any important enterprise, responsibility reaches from top to bottom of the organisation, starting with the patron, if there is one. Some patrons are wonderfully committed, hardworking and effective: where they have been told to act, and are invited to do so, they know their tasks and are co-operative in them. Others in this position do not know their tasks, will not co-operate and are ineffectual when they try, for example, to bring together a possible nucleus of early leaders.

There are obvious difficulties in removing and replacing an established, non-functioning patron, especially if they are royal or sub-royal, but these are important roles not to be given away and wasted, which they too often are.

There are some very fine functioning presidents and vice-presidents – roles that can be used to retain involvement of key people beyond their most active period or to strengthen the organisation's networks for contacts and influence. However, some people at this level are only nominally engaged: in theory, they give weight and credibility to the organisation, but they have no willingness to act for it; they may often not know what organisations they represent, having taken on presidency of so many.

Trustees

The more significant opportunities, and problems, usually arise with the trustees. In law, trustees have inalienable responsibilities, although they can delegate powers. They control the organisation's performance and destiny, unless the Charity Commission intervenes. A new regime for charities' fundraising may increase their timidity and fear of risk.

Generalisations about trustees are impossible. One chairman of trustees known to the author heads a major company, is a highly respected, well-known philanthropist and has great influence with and through his contacts. He is also visionary: where one particular plan hesitated short of the ideal, as a result of internal reactions to it, he thrust it forward to the point it should reach.

In some instances, the trustees have been selected as specialists in a medical or academic or arts field or as representatives of the disadvantaged people served, their carers or their families. These trustees are unlikely to have the expertise appropriate for a major funding development exercise, and it may be necessary, in these circumstances, to create a separate but related body. These are blameless problems created as an organisation considers its big strategy. Where the trustees have been appointed simply because they are friends of existing trustees or friends of their friends, however, there can be serious problems. This quite often happens with major national or regional organisations, where trusteeship or membership of board or council confers specious glory, or where the chair has been passed from generation to generation in a family, sometimes for more than a hundred years. If such an arrangement is compounded by ignorance about the services or cause, lack of vision, aversion to all risk, a fundamental distaste for fundraising – then the effects can be harmful to staff, but also, most critically, to the people served. In one such example, no one dared contradict or remove the noble founder and chair, although staff and advisors knew the delivery of more adequate services depended on this. The founder's stupidity and her underlings' (as she perceived them) timidity prevailed. She would not budge.

Trustees need to be selected with clear task descriptions and appointed because of their knowledge and skills. Within a clear strategy, their responsibilities and the work and time required of them should be defined, and they should be aware what these are. Trustees need training and should be appointed more selectively. I shall return to this.

Senior management

If the strategy has a straightforward financial objective relating to services, senior managers must at least resource and support it. Where the top management does not include fundraising and promotion expertise (a situation often met in smaller organisations), then the strategy must allow for clear explanation, even formal instruction, backed by reassurance and regular updates on progress.

The situation is more acute if the strategy entails radical new directions with a major uplift in funds. In that situation, a new spirit may have to permeate the organisation, involving line managers and staff as well as the directorate. Here management includes the management of change, and energetic, convincing leadership is required. Such leadership is often, but by no means always, given; the strategy can run into serious difficulty if it is regarded with fundamental scepticism by the directorate. There are exceptions: in one such example, a strategy succeeded through the leadership of the finance director while the chief executive remained critical and unhelpful. Normally, however, success demands unqualified commitment of senior management's energy and will.

Education, training and personnel

One of the improvements in the not-for-profit sector over the past decade has been in the provision of training, education and accredited qualifications in management, marketing and fundraising for not-for-profit organisations. Providers have included the Institute of Fundraising, the Open, South Bank and City Universities, such specialists as the Council for the Advancement and Support of Education (CASE) and the Directory of Social Change. There has been a programme for chief executives included in the Institute of Fundraising's yearly convention, and there have been courses for trustees. The International Workshop has expanded from a yearly gathering in Holland to the provision of worldwide training services.

Such expansion has inevitably let in an element of charlatanism, with ill-qualified pundits offering courses which would show the ways to fundraising riches. As the numbers attending the main events have increased, there has been a tendency to rate entertainment value over content, style over substance. Since people will stay away if bored, there is no grave harm in that. However, even at the most reputable gatherings, the same tendency has let in teaching which is factually and operationally wrong, for example, on fundraising with major companies and trusts and with rich individuals.

A contributory factor to this may be found in what has happened with fundraising or development staff over the same period. Here again, as a result of more enlightened policies and the improvements in training mentioned above, the quality of middle management has increased. This is now a sector of activity that meets professional standards and has measurable skills. It has even won a degree of public recognition, particularly from legislators and regulators, again largely through the work of the Institute of Fundraising. There is still a distance to be travelled before fundraising wins due recognition from other publics of importance to it: for example, from those in social work, the arts or academia who become directors of organisations, or those from the sectors of society (the disadvantaged and their carers, as well as the great and good) from which trustees are drawn. Progress will be made towards such recognition over time, even allowing for the still widespread distaste felt towards asking for money, and sometimes for the money culture itself. This recognition will happen as the quality and performance of people working in fundraising are acknowledged.

It is here, however, that a problem remains. At least in some technical fields, the improvements that have taken place in the middle of the organisations have yet to reach the top. It is extremely difficult to find good staff at senior levels, for example, to manage major support programmes. The qualities that people need to operate at this level do not include social or economic backgrounds (Old Etonians do not necessarily make successful major support fundraisers); they do include tact, intelligence, confidence, an understanding of the ways decision makers think and of corporate functionings and, critically, the character to win and hold the confidence of most prospects and supporters. One person is unlikely to be universally acceptable, but this may be compensated for by senior management and the volunteer leadership. For whatever reason, however, there is a scarcity of senior, successful people in this activity of major support – so teaching passes to people who lack successful experience at the higher levels of funding and who have not understood how it works. Damagingly misleading (if entertaining) teaching is one result, and the problem is compounded.

The National Lottery: flawed provider

Supporting Millennium enterprises and exacerbating the problems is our wonderful, welcome Lottery. It is making possible many otherwise unachievable, precious achievements, but the operations of the boards have been wayward and strange. During the last stages of a successful application to the Heritage Fund, it seemed they were try-ing to eliminate candidates through attrition, giving a day or two for producing new cashflows and estimates. If that was not deliberate and unreasonably demanding, it was inefficient. More critical is the issue of matching funding. While it may be reasonable that the boards demand a degree of matching funding, this demand is at pre-sent unrealistically imposed and against formulae (50 per cent, 65 per cent, 75 per cent, 90 per cent) which are only partially valid and too dogmatically applied.

The requirement for partnership funding can be met without crisis by projects backed by local authorities and some larger institutions – although some university-based projects may fail as a result of cut-backs. More schemes may fail, however, because the conditions imposed on offers of support are unrealistic. There are many situa-tions in which fundraising cannot start in earnest before the offer is confirmed and a contract agreed. Friends may have been gathered, and some sources provisionally engaged; but, if a Lottery application is in progress, many prospective funders and advocates want to wait on its conclusive outcome. Indeed, a foundation that made its grant conditional on Lottery funding later withdrew its offer of partnership support from applicants, because it had been overwhelmed by them.

The Lottery is changing philosophies and patterns of grant-making. Where the fundraising has to start from the date a Lottery grant is conditionally offered, the situation is daunting: twelve months for an organisation with no fundraising track record, and therefore no skilled staff and no existing supporters or advocates, to raise multi-ples of £1 million, and with uncertainty still surrounding the offer. Put this in its wider context of a general increase in fundraising com-petition, and there is a fresh swarm of urgent petitions for leadership and partnership funds, many from organisations without experience or sound organisational foundations on which they can build.

In this way the Lottery is increasing competition for funds at a time when competition is more intense than ever. It is changing the pat-terns of support from all kinds of sources to not-for-profit organisa-tions in ways that cannot yet be adequately charted and will for long remain unpredictable. Meanwhile, by imposing partnership condi-tions according to rigid formulae, it has lumbered many organisa-tions it judged worthy with challenges they are unlikely to meet.

Apart from reconsideration of the Lottery's processes, there needs to be change in the requirements for partnership funding. Can an organisation, starting from scratch, reasonably be expected to raise multiples of £1 million at all? Even more improbably, within a year?

Yet, if inception is delayed, costs will significantly increase, as a result of standard inflation and inflation induced by the Lottery itself. So, should the proportions of funding to be raised from organisations be lowered in some instances, even if a degree of partnership funding, however small, continues to be expected from all of those supported? The requirements for partnership funding are currently unrealistic and must certainly have been imposed without consulting experienced and knowledgeable fundraisers. They need to be reconsidered.

Is it inevitable that funds formerly designated for the Millennium will be diverted to supplement taxation?

New Labour: a new context for fundraising

The foreword to *Present Alms: On the Corruption of Philanthropy* (Mullin, 1980), considered the likely impact of Margaret Thatcher's new government: 'None of the changes (in fiscal policies) alters my basic arguments, although they have at least postponed the incarnation of the mono-policied state. It still has to be seen whether the new government will introduce the measures, consistent with their philosophy, which would give charities greater opportunity for vigorous growth and development.'

They did, considerably beyond the author's expectations.

Measures introduced by New Labour have also exceeded my expectations. In a policy document, *Building the Future Together*, published in March 1997, the Labour Party repeatedly endorsed independence for the voluntary sector, recognising 'the riches and diversity of independent organisations and their potential'. The government was responsible, it said, for 'nurturing a vibrant and creative voluntary sector'. To achieve this, Labour would create 'a new settlement between government and the voluntary sector'. Labour would establish a 'national compact' with the voluntary sector, in partnership and consultation with it. This would not be 'contract culture' but 'partnership culture'. The compact would be overseen by 'a task force of ministers, chaired by a senior cabinet minister'; because 'the voluntary sector is central to our vision of a shareholder society' and 'creating a shareholder society is about recreating a civic society'.

That puts the words but not the policies in place. Happily, the Labour statement resisted a recommendation of the Deakin Report, 1996 that there should be 'a single definition of charity' and saw the voluntary sector as standing apart from party politics. It is to be hoped that there is no threat of returning to bad old ways when it says Labour would respect 'the right of voluntary organisations to campaign and to voice the needs of those they serve within the terms of their charitable objects'. More ominously, for reasons we will discuss presently, the document said that charity law would be reviewed 'in the light of current developments in Europe'. There was passing reference to support for the voluntary sector 'from a variety of sources, including public subscription and individual giving, sponsorship and support from business and private trusts' as well as from governments and the EU. Non-statutory funding was recognised as 'an essential strength of the voluntary sector'. There was no mention of fiscal policy relating to charities and little on policy generally, beyond the rhetoric of 'new settlements', 'compacts', 'partnerships' and 'stakeholders'.

The not-for-profit sector has been regarded more favourably than it was by New Labour's more explicitly socialist predecessors, one of whom declared in a debate on *Present Alms* that 'commerce and industry, conventionally organised, in ideology and in daily practice, have nothing to offer to a socialist analysis of the issues that concern us' and 'widespread appeal to individuals necessarily dilutes information and analysis to a lowest common denominator'. There has been no return to such malice.

At least four prominent new ministers moved into Parliament straight from the voluntary sector – Clare Short, Harriet Harman, Frank Field and Nick Raynsford. Frank Field, an early casualty and a realist thinker, said in a recent interview: 'Our job now is to show how self-interest – a natural and wholesome instinct, the greatest driving force in all of us – can also promote the common good.'

Gordon Brown in fact initiated a drive to reinvigorate charitable service, bringing to mind, in Frank Prochaska's words, '. . . working-class traditions of charity, which were once a bulwark of welfare' (British Academy lecture, 8 February 2001). The tax regime for fundraising, as an enabling factor not a motive for giving, has been improved so that it at least matches the regime in the USA. This applies across the full range, from payroll giving to gifts of shares and legacies. Gift Aid has removed the complications of the covenant system. There is even recent provision to claim tax reliefs retrospectively, if a donor who last year paid higher-rate tax is not this year paying at the higher rate. All this creates a very positive environment for fundraising.

There are negatives as well as positives in the situation. Individuals and companies are paying extraordinarily high taxes. National Insurance, increased in the recent budget, is a tax from which gifts to charities do not benefit. Indeed, it is a new burden charities must bear. Taxes on dividends reduce the incomes of grant-making trusts and of charities as they do of pension funds. Harm from the change to advance Corporation Tax remains. Despite rhetoric to the contrary, small businesses pay punitive taxes, having to find one-and-a-half years' tax from one year's income. Although, at the upper levels, incomes are increasing, taxpayers with more modest incomes are suffering.

The reasons why New Labour reverted to Old Labour policies of high taxation for the middle classes – or ordinary donors – are not dishonourable. There are huge demands for the Health Service and Education, if these are to be funded mainly from taxation. At the same time, spending on Defence may have to be raised; and the Unions continue opposing almost all forms of PPF. This means that, while the tax regime may favour giving, direct and indirect taxes reduce the amount an ordinary wage earner can give to charity. As the proportion of old people in the population continues to rise, pressures to save rather than to give will increase. And, as costs for the provision of care for older people rise, while state provision for them declines, there will be less funding available for charity legacies (although increases in property prices may help compensate this). At the same time, because of statutory regulations, care homes for older people are closing, where they cannot be run economically while meeting statutory regulations, so that new demands for funds are created.

Fundraising for state schools will surely continue; as it will for cottage hospitals, scanners, and ancillary health services. Will the tax benefits of the public schools be allowed to continue? Will arts funding be directed away from centres of excellence and glory to the drabness of community arts? The present Minister does not discriminate between them, so will funds be taken from opera, ballet, great orchestras, and expensive exhibitions and given to populist art forms, and to soccer, athletics and swimming? Presumably funding stringencies for higher education will continue to affect students, teaching, research, buildings and plant – demanding voluntary fundraising.

The Institute of Fundraising (formerly the Institute of Charity Fundraising Managers) has over recent years made a main contribution in establishing standards for different forms of fundraising. This was appropriate because, unlike NCVO and the Charity Commission, the Institute understands fundraising. As new regulations for fundraising were awaited from government, it was hoped there would be a real move to de-regulation or at least an increase in self-regulation, making the 1993 Charities Act, to some degree at least, redundant.

In September 2002, the Government Strategy Unit published its *Private Action, Public Benefit*, proposing a future regime for charity fundraising. It is a typical New Labour document, proposing a new body to police fundraising and steps for 'measuring and improving organisational performance'. A glance at education and health provision should provoke a shudder here. The argument for creating a new 'body concerned solely with fundraising' is based on a logical *non sequitur*. It argues that 'because of the numerous methods used to fundraise . . . there would therefore be great benefit in having a single point of contact for information about regulatory requirements for fundraising'. There is no 'therefore'. The new body's board would consist of people and bodies from the sector, from government and home office, and people from outside government, home office and the sector. It is not clear how these people would be selected or what would be the terms of their appointment. The Institute is acknowledged (its board is elected) but will, apparently, be sidelined.

The new body would deal with complaints from the public. It would 'develop an overall Code of Good Fundraising Practice and more specific codes covering different aspects of fundraising which go beyond the basic minimum standards set down by law'. I am baffled to think what an *overall* code might look like; but it would require a *Guide for the Perplexed* to interpret its ramifications. No real case is made for a new body or code, when there are others in place that could, with resources and adjustment, carry out its functions. I would apply Ockham's razor here. Worse, the proposal is that the new body should be funded 'by a small levy on donated income': a new tax on donors and their gifts!

The 'new fundraising body' would be intended 'to develop the self-regulatory initiative' for the sector. But there is an explicit threat: 'if self regulation is not successful, the Home Secretary should have a back-up power to introduce a system of statutory regulations'. That would be dire.

Charity fundraising will be on trial under increased self-regulation. Benchmarks for fundraising, developed by the Institute and Adrian Sargeant at Henley, and acknowledged in the report, will be established to measure the cost-effectiveness of fundraising and the efficiency of fundraising management. There will be kitemarks for efficiency and effectiveness; perhaps a Quality Mark tied to Best Value Performance Indicators. The new body will establish and monitor those standards. This is excellent. But if, within a given period, the sector does not perform to its own set standards, more stringent regulation will be imposed from outside. One peril is that misguided or ignorant concentration on fundraising ratios will underpin unjustified criticism. Ratios that apply to income-generation do not apply, for example, to organisations which must have in reserve funds committed to long-term research; and investment needed to develop new fundraising sources show lower yields in their early years than expenditure on established sources. In addition to the tasks directly involved in such self-regulation, huge educational and communications exercises will be entailed. All publics must be convinced that the standards set are apt and that they have been achieved. More problematically, trustees and senior, non-fundraising managers must be educated so that they understand the rationale for these standards and the implications for their application. In other words, there must be a transformation in understanding for most trustees and many charity managers. This is an undertaking for the whole sector.

European perils

The most serious challenges to not-for-profit activity in the UK are likely to come from elsewhere, especially if Labour behaves with short-sighted compliance towards Europe.

European data-protection legislation, for example, would grievously have damaged direct marketing in the UK by imposing the kinds of regime applied in countries whose not-for-profit sectors are less thriving, or thriving in different ways. The damage was prevented, voluntary sector representatives playing key roles in this. European regimes can be extremely restrictive. For example, one advertising campaign's financial press advertisements in Germany were allowed to claim nothing about the financial instrument being promoted (the campaign referred to these advertisements as Tombstones). The UK was late to notice the data-protection legislation, and its implications. The woman who was drafting the directive had not even considered not-for-profit organisations at that stage. Today there is a similar lack of attention in the UK, or of awareness in the European Commission, about the issues at stake. These issues are even more fundamental now than then.

There seems to be a combination of ignorance, indifference, neglect and lack of serious anticipation about things to come. We seem to suffer such disasters by default. A similar situation may already be developing for not-for-profit organisations to that which has already affected the art world. Did the art market need to move, by European decree, from London to Switzerland and New York, with no significant gain for many artists? The danger is always that regulations will drag organisations down to the lowest common denominators, and the least advantageous regimes.

In the UK at the moment, there is well-established legislation for trusts, dating back centuries, which in its adapted forms operates quite satisfactorily for not-for-profit organisations here. There is also remarkably favourable tax treatment for both donors and recipients of funds. The tax system has improved well beyond many people's expectations over the past decade, with persuasion from CAF (the Charities Aid Foundation), among others. Recent papers from Brussels, however, threaten the independence and tax treatment of not-for-profit organisations across Europe, again imposing the least favourable and most restrictive regimes. They would bring in legislation from a tradition of Roman law to bring 'associations' – which cover 'charities' and other not-for-profit organisations – under the control of governments and public authorities. As concepts of 'government' are dissolved in the European Community, this will mean control by the undemocratic Commission and its unelected, unaccountable bodies. There is a fundamental contradiction here of voluntary organisation and initiative, which would destroy the independence of the voluntary sector, making it subservient to the state. But who is paying attention to this threat?

Adapting to changing circumstances

Charity fundraisers have to be constantly alert for changes in their context for fundraising, and responsive to them. Changes in government policies and provisions inevitably affect charities, which exist to respond to needs in the community. So shortfalls and inadequacies in services for underprovided older and sick people, for lone parents and their children, for homeless people, for immigrants and refugees and a host of other causes become challenges for charities, perhaps requiring enhanced fundraising. The government's inadequate funding of universities and research, as of healthcare and education generally, leave continuing demands. Over the years ahead, charities as well as governments will have to respond to massive demands from Africa and other parts of the developing world.

There have also been changes in the context for fundraising within the sector. It is now a truism that competition in fundraising has become increasingly intense, in the targets set and the range of techniques being used. The sector itself has changed over the past fifteen years. Then there were not the professional bodies and courses and standards, the journals, the opportunities for networking, the salaries and career opportunities, which we have now. There are more, better-qualified fundraisers in the field. But excellence had not increased in proportion to the improvements in qualifications. There is widespread mediocrity and pusillanimity in undertaking challenging enterprises and in pursuing strategies to deliver them. I have seen this particularly in some senior fundraisers' incompetence in dealing at the highest levels with major corporate and individual prospects. Evidently, a strategic plan must allow for the competence of the staff available to implement it.

Conclusion: the need to develop strategic thinking

What has all this to do with strategies for fundraising?

Even if fundraisers may not be expected to be expert strategic planners, they should be expected to think strategically. This means, among other things, that they can see beyond the situation immediately facing them and assess it in context. Beyond the horizon are the returns on investment, closer and more supportive contacts with main supporters, even higher targets and an organisation with greatly enhanced capacities for service. Around the corner are grave shocks and possible serendipity. The fundraiser must have the flexibility to adapt plans if necessary, and the strength to maintain them through difficulties or to abort them – whichever may be right. A strategic fundraiser must be able to articulate and even reinterpret an organisation's vision, thrusting ahead to conclusions on mission and operations.

Not-for-profit initiative is essential to a thriving civil society. Its funding, in balance with or opposed to statutory provision, must give the organisations involved significant independence from government. There must be scope for challenges, contradictions, and for alternative provision of services. In the arts and academia, there must be no subservience to the censor or to state control. Not-for-profit agencies' strategies for funding must be far-sighted, allowing for the alternatives and external factors, and they must be expertly designed and implemented, fully capable of delivering the resources needed.

To repeat, why is all this necessary?

Because these strategies are needed to realise the societies in which we choose to live.

Appendices

Appendix 1 Typical job description for a development director

1 The development director's overall responsibilities will be concerned with the implementation and administration of the fundraising strategy. The director will report to the director and trustees and to any authorised persons or groups authorised by them to take action for the appeal, as occasion requires. In detail, the related tasks will include:

a *Implementation of the strategy for the realisation of this support.*

b *The maintenance of research files on prospective supporters to include individuals, companies and trusts, the Lottery and other UK and overseas sources.*

c *The enlistment of appropriate individuals to assist the organisation in its fundraising activities.*

d *The organisation and servicing of meetings, briefings and other contacts with voluntary helpers, groups and prospective supporters.*

e *The preparation, production and dissemination of related promotional materials, communications and information for the staff, volunteers, groups and prospective supporters concerned.*

f *The initiation and oversight of fundraising with prosperous, popular and other segments of prospects, and of special events and activities relating to all aspects of the appeal.*

g *The initiation and oversight of related publicity, through public relations, advertising and other means.*

h *The management of gift aid, covenant, legacy and other on-going programmes.*

i *The establishment of methods to monitor performance in relation to the timetables and targets set by the organisation and authorised committees, and to report to them on these matters.*

j *The administration of the office and records and the supervision of any staff concerned in the appeal.*

k *The development director will be expected to maintain continuing vigilance, initiative, resourcefulness and enterprise in furthering the interests of the organisation and in fostering its relationships with other organisations, groups and individuals capable of contributing to its work and development.*

2 The organisation should undertake to provide its development director with the co-operation and support required for the accomplishment of the responsibilities outlined above.

3 It is the task of such a director to articulate, even reinterpret, the vision, carrying it through to its conclusions for mission and for operations.

Appendix 2 Model timetable for a strategy embracing major, prosperous and popular support

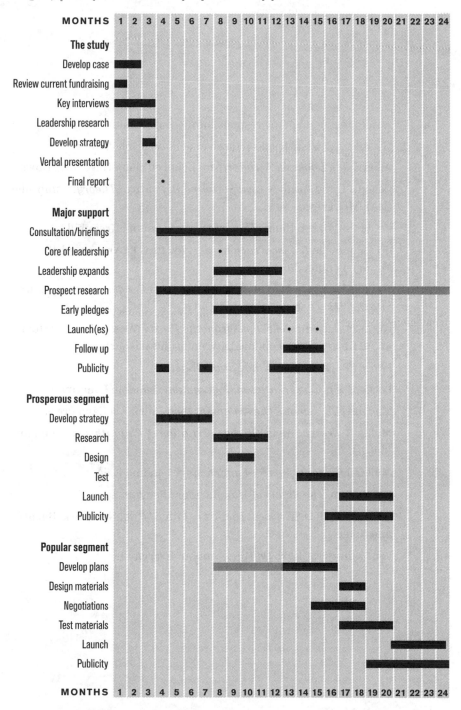

References

Alberti *Ten Books on Architecture* (Leoni edition). New York: Dover.

Cohen J L and Arato A *Civil Society and Political Theory*. Cambridge (MA): MIT Press.

de Jomini, Baron Henri *The Art of War*. London: Greenhill.

de Tocqueville A *Democracy in America* (tr G Lawrence, ed JP Mayer). London: Fontana.

Deakin, Nicholas *Meeting the challenge of change: voluntary action into the 21st century*. London. NCVO.

Gramsci, Antonio *Selections from the Prison Notebooks* (ed Q Hoare and G Have Smith). London: Lawrence and Wishart.

Labour Party *Building the Future Together*.

Locke, John *Two Treaties of Government*. London: Everyman.

Machiavelli, Niccolò *The Art of War*. New York: Da Capo Press.

Mullin R *Present Alms: On the Corruption of Philanthropy*. London: Phlogiston.

Mullin R *Foundations for Fundraising*. London: ICFA.

Paine, Tom *The Rights of Man*. London: Penguin.

Tzu, Sun (tr R D Sawyer). *The Art of War 500 BC*. New York: Barnes and Noble.

von Clausewitz, Karl *On War*. London: Everyman.

About the Directory of Social Change

The Directory of Social Change (DSC) is an independent voice for positive social change, set up in 1975 to help voluntary organisations become more effective. It does this by providing practical, challenging and affordable information and training to meet the current, emerging and future needs of the sector.

DSC's main activities include:

- researching and publishing reference guides and handbooks;
- providing practical training courses;
- running conferences and briefing sessions;
- organising Charityfair, the biggest annual form for the sector;
- encouraging voluntary groups to network and share information;
- campaigning to promote the interests of the voluntary sector as a whole.

The Directory of Social Change

24 Stephenson Way
London
NW1 2DP

Federation House
Hope Street
Liverpool
L1 9BW

website: www.dsc.org.uk
e-mail: info@dsc.org.uk

Publications and subscriptions
tel: 020 7209 5151
fax: 020 7391 4804

Publicity
tel: 020 7391 4900

Research
tel: 020 7391 4880
0151 708 0136

Courses and conferences
tel: 020 7209 4949
0151 708 0117

Charityfair
tel: 020 7209 4949
020 7209 1015 (exhibitors)

Other publications from the Directory of Social Change

All the following titles are published by the Directory of Social Change, unless otherwise stated, and are available from:

Publications Department

Directory of Social Change

24 Stephenson Way

London

NW1 2DP

Call 020 7209 5151 or e-mail books@dsc.org.uk for more details and for a free publications list, which can also be viewed at the DSC website (www.dsc.org.uk). Prices were correct at the time of going to press but may be subject to change.

The fundraising series

Published in association with CAF and the Institute of Fundraising.

Community Fundraising
The effective use of volunteer networks

Edited by Harry Brown

Volunteer networks are a key resource for fundraising, but are often not appreciated as they should be. This new title demonstrates how to make the most of your volunteers. It covers:

- what community fundraising is
- why people volunteer, the value of volunteers and staff attitudes to volunteers
- the recruitment, retention and development of volunteers
- the management of staff working with volunteers
- case studies from a range of different types of charities – and what can be learned from these.

192 pages, 1st edition, 2002

ISBN 1 900360 98 5 £19.95

Corporate Fundraising

Edited by Valerie Morton

Corporate Fundraising is a fast-moving area and the second edition of this book has been completely revised and updated to include:

- new chapters on corporate social responsibility and on evaluation
- a new appendix on the internet
- a revised section on the legal and tax framework
- a range of new case studies from major charities and companies such as NCH, Diabetes UK, One2One and the Mencap–Transco partnership.

The book continues to offer a comprehensive overview, detailing the variety of ways in which charities and companies may work together to mutual advantage, and addressing key issues around ethics and standards.

200 pages, 2nd edition, 2002

ISBN 1 903991 00 5 £19.95

Fundraising Databases

Peter Flory

Computerised databases are an essential tool for fundraising, but fundraisers often lack the technical background to help them choose a suitable database and use it effectively. This new book provides a clear framework for making and implementing such decisions. It explains what a database is and how it works, before going on to examine:

- why fundraisers need a database
- the functions of a fundraising database
- future trends

Case studies from a range of charities are used throughout to illustrate the points made.

160 pages, 1st edition, 2001

ISBN 1 900360 91 8 £19.95

Legacy Fundraising
The Art of Seeking Bequests

Edited by Sebastian Wilberforce

This unique guide to one of the most important sources of revenue for charities has been revised and updated to include new material on telephone fundraising, forecasting income, and profiling. It also contains the full text of the new Institute of Fundraising Code of Practice on legacy fundraising. Contributions from a range of experts in the field cover both strategy and techniques, and are complemented by perspectives from donors and their families. The breadth of coverage and accessible style ensure that, whether you are an established legacy fundraiser or new to the field, this book is a must.

224 pages, 2nd edition, 2001

ISBN 1 900360 93 4 £19.95

Trust Fundraising

Edited by Anthony Clay

This book outlines a variety of approaches to trusts that will save trustees' time and ensure greater success for fundraising by:

- emphasising the importance of research and maintaining records;
- demonstrating the value of using contacts and a personal approach;
- reinforcing the need for detailed planning of a strategy;
- showing how to make an approach to trusts, and how not to;
- stressing the importance of continued contact with a trust.

152 pages, 1st edition, 1999

ISBN 1 85934 069 5 £19.95

Other titles from DSC

The Complete Fundraising Handbook

Nina Botting & Michael Norton

Published in association with the Institute of Fundraising

For the new edition of this ever-popular title, the information has been completely updated and also reorganised, making it even easier to use. It is now divided into three parts, covering:

- fundraising principles and strategies
- sources of fundraising – including individual donors, grant-making trusts, companies, and central and local government
- fundraising techniques – from house-to-house collections and challenge events, to direct mail and capital appeals.

Illustrated with case studies throughout, the book provides a wealth of practical advice on every aspect of fundraising for charity.

368 pages, 4th edition, 2001

ISBN 1 900360 84 5 £16.95

The Grant-making Trusts CD-ROM

Software development by FunderFinder

Published in association with CAF

This CD-ROM combines the trusts databases of the Directory of Social Change and the Charities Aid Foundation to provide the most comprehensive and up-to-date information ever on grant-making trusts. The improved search facilities ensure fast, easy and effective searching across the whole database.

Contents

- Around 4,000 trusts as listed in the *Directory of Grant Making Trusts*, the three *Guides to Major Trusts*, the four *Guides to Local Trusts*, and the *Guide to Scottish Trusts*
- Full commentary from DSC guide displayed if available
- DGMT entry displayed for smaller trusts where full commentary is unavailable.

Search facilities

- Powerful combined search by geographical area, type of activity and type of beneficiary
- Search by name of trust, location, type of grant or trustee improved for 2002
- Search by key word.

Software

- PC format only
- Runs on Windows 95 and above
- Network capability
- 'Getting started' tutorial
- Hyperlinks to trust websites or e-mail
- Facility to bookmark selected trusts, add your own notes, print individual entries and tag for printing or export.

Single CD-ROM, 2nd edition, 2002

ISBN 1 903991 12 9 £110 + VAT = £129.25

£80 + VAT = £94 for existing users

Website: trustfunding.org.uk

www.trustfunding.org.uk contains all the same data as the Grant-making Trusts CD-ROM, but will be regularly updated throughout the year.

- Search on geographical area, type of activity or type of beneficiary; by name of trust, name of trustee, type of grant, or location; key word search.
- Browser requirements: Internet Explorer version 4 and above or Netscape version 4 and above.
- Hyperlinks to trust websites or e-mail.
- Facility to print individual trust records and tag contact and address details for export.

Annual subscription

Charities and voluntary organisations: £110 + VAT = £129.25

Statutory and commercial organisations: £150 + VAT = £176.25

Once your payment has been received, you will be sent a user name and password, which you can use to access the site from any computer. You can change your password if you wish. Visit the site to see a demonstration.

Managing Without Profit

Mike Hudson

The key elements of successful management for non-profit-making organisations are covered in the second edition of this popular title. Managers from voluntary, arts, housing and campaigning organisations will learn how to:

- establish strong boards
- strengthen strategic management
- develop a mission
- manage and inspire people
- create a learning organisation
- manage change.

440 pages, 2nd edition, 1999

ISBN 1 903991 28 5   £12.99

About CAF

CAF, Charities Aid Foundation, is a registered charity with a unique mission – to increase the substance of charity in the UK and overseas. It provides services that are both charitable and financial which help donors make the most of their giving and charities make the most of their resources.

As an integral part of its activities, CAF works to raise standards of management in voluntary organisations. This includes the making of grants by its own Grants Council, sponsorship of the Charity Annual Report and Accounts Awards, seminars, training courses and the Charities Annual Conference, the largest regular gathering of key people from within the voluntary sector. In addition, Charitynet (www.charitynet.org) is now established as the leading Internet site on voluntary action.

For decades, CAF has led the way in developing tax-effective services to donors, and these are now used by more than 250,000 individuals and 2,000 of the UK's leading companies, between them giving £150 million each year to charity. Many are also using CAF's CharityCard, the world's first debit card designed exclusively for charitable giving. CAF's unique range of investment and administration services for charities includes the CafCash High Interest Cheque Account, two common investment funds for longer-term investment and a full appeals and subscription management service.

CAF's activities are not limited to the UK, however. Increasingly, CAF is looking to apply the same principles and develop similar services internationally, in its drive to increase the substance of charity across the world. CAF has offices and sister organisations in the United States, Bulgaria, South Africa, Russia, India and Brussels.

CAF Research is a leading source of information and research on the voluntary sector's income and resources. Its annual publication, *Dimensions of the Voluntary Sector*, provides year-on-year updates and its Research Report series covers a wide range of topics, including costs benchmarking, partnership resources, and trust and company funding. More details on research and publications may be found on www.CAFonline.org/research

For more information about CAF, please visit www.CAFonline.org/

About the Institute of Fundraising

The Institute of Fundraising is the only organisation that exists to represent and support the professional interests of fundraisers at all levels. The Institute of Fundraising welcomes membership applications from all those working in a fundraising role or consultancy practice – from those new to the profession to those with many years' experience.

The benefits to be gained are available to all. As a professional body, the Institute of Fundraising assists its members at every stage and in every facet of their professional development. It provides opportunities for continuing professional education, a forum for discussion on issues of common concern, a source of information and a point of contact with other professionals.

The Institute of Fundraising Certificate of Membership is evidence of the holder's commitment to the Codes and the professional standards set by the Institute. Since membership is individual, it is fully transferable if you change your job. In liaison with other umbrella groups, the Institute of Fundraising also represents members' interests to charities, government, the media and to the public.

The Institute of Fundraising is supported financially by many charities who recognise the importance and needs of the organisation, having become affiliates of its Charitable Trust. Fundraising staff of these affiliated charities enjoy reduced subscription fees. Through its members, the Institute of Fundraising liaises worldwide with allied organisations, such as the National Society of Fundraising Executives in the USA and the Australian Institute of Fundraising, and is represented on the World Fundraising Council.

The Institute of Fundraising aims, through its Trust, to further knowledge, skills and effectiveness in the field of fundraising. It serves the interests of its members, the professional fundraisers, and through them, the interests of charitable bodies and donors. The

Institute of Fundraising aims to set and develop standards of fundraising practice which encompass:

- growth in the funds and resources available for charitable expenditure;
- thorough knowledge of proven fundraising techniques;
- new fundraising opportunities;
- cost effectiveness;
- strict adherence to the law;
- accountability.

Institute of Fundraising Codes of Practice, Guidance Notes, and the Charity Donors' Rights Charter

The Institute of Fundraising Codes of Practice and Guidance Notes aim to act as a guide to best practice for fundraisers, and as a benchmark against which the public can measure fundraising practice. They cover a wide variety of issues and aim to address both practical and ethical concerns.

The Codes are drawn up by working parties composed of representatives of the various interested constituents in a particular field, and undergo an extensive consultation process through the charities affiliated to the Institute of Fundraising, regulators and government.

As new areas of interest are identified, so new Codes are drafted, often at the rate of two or three each year, under the supervision of the Institute of Fundraising Standards Committee. Both Charity Commission and Home Office are represented on this committee and play a major role in the development of any new work.

The Codes are endorsed and observed by fundraising organisations throughout the UK. They are recognised as demonstrating the commitment of the voluntary sector to the promotion of best practice.

The Charity Donors' Rights Charter has been developed as a compact between fundraisers and the supporters of the organisations for which they work. It aims to address the expectations that a supporter has of the organisation they give to, and to articulate the commitment the sector makes to them.

Codes of Practice

Charity Challenge Events
UK Charity Challenge Events
Fundraising in Schools
House to House Collections
Telephone Recruitment of Collectors
Personal Solicitation of Committed Gifts
Legacy Fundraising

Outbound Telephone Support
Payroll Giving
Reciprocal Charity Mailings

Guidance Notes

The Acceptance and Refusal of Donations
Data Protection Act 1998
The Management of Static Collection Boxes
The Use of Chain Letters as a Fundraising Technique
UK Charity Challenge Events

New Codes for 2001

Raffles and Lotteries
Fundraising on the Internet

Copies of the Codes of Practice, Guidance Notes and Charity Donors'
Rights Charter may be obtained from the Institute of Fundraising at:

Institute of Fundraising
5th Floor
Market Towers
1 Nine Elms Lane
London SW8 5NQ
Tel: 020 7627 3436

Or from:
enquiries@institute-of-fundraising.org.uk

Index